The Dancers Own Cookbook

Flora Dulen
1988

THE DANCERS OWN COOKBOOK

Flora Duley

REMOUS

First published in England in 1988 by
Remous Limited, Sherborne, Dorset

ISBN 0 951351 3 0 3 Paperback
ISBN 0 951351 3 1 1 Hardback

Original paintings and drawings by Robert Heindel on the front cover and pages 98 and 188 reproduced by kind permission of The Obsession of Dance Company, 10 Bellevue Road, Wandsworth Common, London SW17 7EB.
Telephone 01-767 4688.

Line drawings elsewhere are by Alice Finch-Hatton, Ashley Thompson, Jim Penwarden and Lenny Copeland.

Book Layout and Typesetting by Crane/Barnden Limited, Frog Lane, Ilminster, Somerset TA19 0AP.

Printed by Remous Limited, North Street, Milborne Port, Sherborne, Dorset DT9 5ET.

With love
to all my children
Carol, David, James,
Sarah and Giles

COOKERY FOR DANCERS

It has been said that Pavlova's fans boiled her old point shoes and made soup which they drank, such was their admiration for the great dancer.

I am keeping the shoes of today's dancers in the hope that, providing they eat well, they will become the great dancers they are dedicating themselves to be, then I will have the basis for a 'Celebrity Soup'.

PROGRAMME

INTRODUCTION

A dancers second love is usually food, they avidly read recipes and entertain friends. This small book aims to feed sensibly those small but always hungry 'tums' in an economical, balanced and nutritious way, not forgetting the fun side, and banishing that guilty, 'I shouldn't have eaten that' feeling.

My original idea was to put together recipes that would allow for a dancers particular needs: food for stamina, sweet needs, nutrition, economy and keeping slim. I hope I have achieved this.

Having got to know so many of you, students and performers, boys and girls, I have marvelled at your discipline, been horrified at your eating habits, enjoyed your company and dancing, and most of all admired you. You richly deserve your very own cook book. So - Follow my food and ON WITH THE DANCE.

SETTING THE SCENE

The cooking scene, like the stage, needs props and action.

USE METRIC OR IMPERIAL WEIGHTS, DO NOT MIX THE TWO. *(See Conversion Table, page 202).*

Storage: Most dried (and canned) goods have a shelf life of months, and are best kept in tins or plastic boxes. Vegetables and fruit need eating quickly to obtain the best vitamin content. Biscuits, cakes and pastry need airtight containers; separate ones of course. Jams, pickles and sauces keep well for long periods. Butter, margarine, lard, dripping, milk and yogurt need to be kept in the fridge and used within their 'best before' date. Uncooked meat and fish should be kept in the fridge, but away from other cooked foods, and used as soon as possible. Cooked meats last about a week in the fridge and small quantities can be frozen, as long as they have not been frozen before.

Fish. Best eaten as soon as possible, shell fish especially.

Eggs & Cheese are a good standby, they keep well and are very nourishing.

If possible sieve flour before using.

When using egg whites the yolks can be kept in a container in the fridge for about a week.

Cream whisks quicker when it is not too cold.

Quantities. Do not be afraid to halve or quarter quantities in recipes, making sure to reduce cooking times in proportion.

Close at hand — always try to keep: Parsley; fresh can be kept in a glass of water for a week. Chopped up and put in a plastic container it freezes for months.

Garlic, Lemons, Sea Salt, Black Pepper, Nuts, Fresh or Dried Herbs are all extra sources of nourishment and will add flavour and appeal to the humblest dish.

Sprouting Seeds such as Alfalfa, Mung and Aduki are easily grown in pots and are rich in vitamins. Follow the directions given on packet when growing.

When shopping try to find markets, W.I. markets, health shops, delicatessens, bakers, butchers and greengrocers; keep supermarkets for general store shopping. Doing this will enable you to buy fresher, less expensive, additive free foods, which in turn taste better and do you more good.

Some Cooking Terms

Au gratin — food sprinkled with breadcrumbs and butter then browned under the grill.

Baking — cooking by radiated heat in the oven.

Basting — spooning hot fat over meat during cooking to keep moist.

Blanching — to make food white or to preserve its colour, immerse in boiling water for a few minutes.

Blind — Baking pastry without filling (usually needs foil or beans whilst baking).

Braising — a method of cooking. Place food to be cooked on a bed of cut up vegetables, add a little water and cook slowly in a covered pan, the lid should be removed in the last half hour to allow meat to brown.

Caramel — Sugar heated slowly in a thick pan until brown and caramelized.

Casserole — A dish with a tight fitting lid, oven proof, allowing food to be cooked slowly in the oven.

Coat — to cover food evenly with thin coating of, for example, egg, cream or breadcrumbs.

Consommé — A clear soup.

Compôte — Fruit stewed with sugar (polite name for stewed fruit).

Creaming — Working together a mixture of fat and sugar.

Dissolve — To melt solid foods in a liquid — sugar in water is an example.

Dredging — Sprinkling a substance over food. Flour and sugar are both frequently used this way.

Dropping consistency — describes a soft dough mixture.

Duxelles — Savoury mixture of chopped mushrooms and onions, seasoned with salt, pepper and nutmeg.

Entrée — a savoury dish that is usually served before the main dish.

Egg and Crumb — Food dipped into egg then into breadcrumbs or flour before frying.

Filter — Strain through a cloth or filter bag.

Folding in — A method of combining whipped or creamed mixtures with other ingredients, so that air and therefore lightness is retained. A metal spoon is the best implement to use for this folding in action.

Fool — Purée of fruit mixed with cream or custard.

Glaze — Brush over the tops of pies and pastries with a liquid such as egg, or sugar and water - gives a shiny finish.

Knead — To work dough with the knuckles, used for bread and some pastries.

Maigre — A dish without meat.

Marinade — A mixture of oil, wine or vinegar, or lemon juice, herbs and seasoning, in which meat is soaked before cooking.

Parboiling — To half cook food by boiling before continuing the cooking by another method, roast potatoes for example.

Poaching — Cooking food lightly in a liquid, usually water or milk.

Ragôut — A rich stew seasoned and flavoured with wine, tomato and mushrooms.

Roux — Mixture of fat and flour fried together, a basis for sauces.

Rubbing in — A method of rubbing fat into flour.

Reduce — Boiling a mixture rapidly to concentrate the flavour.

Steam — Cooking vegetables or puddings, using a steamer or a colander over a saucepan — not immersed in water. (You can buy folding steamers very reasonably that will fit in a saucepan).

Sauté — To fry gently in fat, usually butter, sauté potatoes are an example.

Seasoned Flour — Flour to which salt and pepper have been added.

Steep — To soak in either hot or cold liquid.

Simmer — To cook in a liquid kept below boiling point.

Basic uses of easily obtained herbs

Basil — Sausages, chicken, tomato and courgette dishes.

Chives — A garnish for meat, fish, salads and savoury butter.

Dill — Use with fish - or as herbal tea.

Fennel — In soup imparts a strong liquorish taste also with veal, pork and fish.

Garlic — A clove goes well and adds distinction to many meat dish, sauces, dressings, and with salads.

Marjoram — Red meat, pizza, liver and poultry.

Parsley — Garnish, parsley butter, salads and sauces.

Rosemary — Lamb and fish.

Sage — Sage and onion stuffing - in boiling bacon, soya beans, lentils and savoury rice.

Tarragon — Excellent for chicken.

Thyme — Good with soup and stuffings, no bouquet garni would be complete without it.

Dried mixed herbs — Very useful for every day cooking in omelettes, pizzas, mince, bolognese, casseroles, stuffings.

Vegetarians

will find many dishes 'just for them' in Act 1 scenes 2, 4, 5 and Variations parts 1, 2 & 3, plus of course all the sweet sections!

Many dancers are vegetarians, or part vegetarians and as long as they eat something from each of the necessary foods to achieve a balanced diet, all is well.

Curtain
— Up —

ACT 1

SCENE 1

CORPS DE CHOCOLATE

NOTES ON CHOCOLATE

Chocolate may be indulged in with an easy conscience, as it provides energy, with little bulk. It is a very good source of iron and a quick 'pick-me-up' BUT too much 'picking-up' can spoil the appetite for more important foods and may also put on extra weight that is not required.

Chocolate should be kept in each room and locker — in case of emergencies!

Chocolate should head your list of necessities to take on tour, to performances, classes, parties, picnics and journeys.

Chocolate CAN be shared.

Chocolate is BAD for self-discipline, waist-lines and complexions.

Chocolate is GOOD for hunger, nerves, consolation, sharing with friends, passing round in class, giving as a good luck present, for grating on to food, in drinks, etc. A big box or bar of chocolate is a great morale booster.

Chocolate bars, boxes or Easter Eggs bought as a present for someone else should NOT be tasted on the way home!

Always serve too much chocolate or fudge sauce to your guests, they will love you forever.

CHOCOLATE IS FOR CHEERING.

ON MELTING CHOCOLATE

1. Always melt chocolate slowly, over a low heat.

2. Grate chocolate, place in heatproof bowl, stand over pan of hot, not boiling water — do make sure no water splashes into chocolate as even a drop of moisture will cause chocolate to stiffen. If it does stiffen a tiny drop of oil may help. White chocolate is susceptible to overheating — needs extra care.

3. Microwave melting — use defrost on low setting. Break chocolate into pieces, place in microwave bowl, cook 1-2 minutes until glossy — can burn easily.

4. Store chocolate in cool, dry place, not fridge, as fluctuations in temperature cause a greyish bloom (due to cocoa butter melting) to appear. Not dangerous but does not look so nice.

WORKING WITH CHOCOLATE

Chocolate Flakes (Caraque)

1. Spread melted chocolate on marble or Formica suface, leave to set hard.

2. Using a sharp knife at a 45 degree angle shave off thin layers of chocolate, forming tight curls. Dust with icing sugar — lovely decoration.

Chocolate Curls

Scrape a vegetable peeler along flat side of a thick bar of chocolate — produces thick, narrow curls.

Chocolate Leaves

1. Pick firm rose leaves — dry with kitchen tissue if damp.

2. Brush veined side with melted chocolate — thickly. Leave to harden. Gently peel away leaf. Do some with dark chocolate, some with white chocolate.

Chocolate Cut Out Shapes

1. Spread melted chocolate thickly onto sheet of waxed paper — leave to set for 1 - 2 hours.

2. Use pastry cutters, or shapes, or cut own designs using sharp knife — lift off with flat knife.

Chocolate Squares — for boxes

1. As for cut out shapes, cut squares of chocolate all same size, leave to harden.

2. Cut squares of sponge cake, coat sides with jam, put square of chocolate on each side.

3. Dab of cream on top of cake, then another square of chocolate at an angle, like a lid.

Chocolate Truffle Cake (rich)

This can be made with either white chocolate or plain dark chocolate.

200g/8oz plain chocolate
500ml/1 pint double cream
1 tsp icing sugar } *for dusting –*
1 tsp cocoa powder } *sieve these 2 together*
Fruit, or nuts of your choice to decorate top
1 plain or chocolate sponge cake (bought or made previously see Page 00)

1 terrine tin 3" x 3" x 11"

Method

1. Line the terrine tin with cling film.
2. Melt chocolate in bowl over hot water (see page 11).
3. Whisk cream until very thick.
4. Add cooled chocolate to cream, mix gently.
5. Pour into lined terrine tin.
6. Cut sponge into size of terrine tin – put on top of cream/choc mix, press down firmly.
7. Place in fridge for 24 hours.

When cold turn out on to serving dish, remove cling film, dust top and sides with premixed cocoa powder and icing sugar.

Decorate top with slices of fruit or nuts.

You can make an economy version of this by using left over stale cake, pressed firmly into any shaped tin, using just 250ml/½ pint double cream and 150g/6oz chocolate.

One Stage Chocolate Cake

150g/6ozs soft margarine
150g/6oz caster sugar
150g/6oz self-raising flour
1½ level tsp baking powder
2 medium eggs
2 tbsp cocoa powder } *blend together*
2 tbsp hot water

Oven: Gas no. 3. 170°C. 325°F.
Two 7" cake tins lined with greaseproof paper.

Method

Put margarine, sugar, flour and baking powder in bowl, mix together. Add chocolate mixture, cream all together. Put half mixture in each tin.

Bake on middle shelf for 20 - 25 minutes.

Icing and Filling

(You can halve these ingredients if less rich filling required).

75g/3ozs soft margarine
230g/8ozs icing sugar
1 heaped tbsp cocoa and 2 tbsp hot water blended together

Mix all ingredients together to form smooth chocolate cream. Sandwich cooled cake with half mixture, spread rest on top. Decorate with chocolate flake.

Millionaires Shortbread

(makes approximately 24)

Base

100g/4ozs butter or margarine
50g/2ozs caster sugar
150g/6ozs flour

Filling

100g/4ozs butter or margarine
100g/4ozs caster sugar
2 tbsp golden syrup
4 tbsp condensed milk

Topping

150g/6ozs dark chocolate
25g/1oz butter

Oven: Gas no. 4. 180°C. 350°F. Approximately 20 minutes.
Cake Tin: 9" x 11"

Method

Base: Cream together butter and sugar, add flour, knead until smooth, press evenly over base of tin.
Bake in preheated oven until crisp and golden. Cool in tin.

Filling: Put all ingredients into a pan, and stir over low heat until melted and smooth. Bring to boil, cook for 5 - 6 minutes until golden caramel colour. Spread over base and leave to cool.

Topping: Melt chocolate in a bowl over hot water. Add butter and stir until dissolved. Spread evenly over base. Leave to set then cut into squares or fingers.

Brownies (makes approximately 12)

100g/4ozs soft margarine
100g/4ozs caster sugar
100g/4ozs self raising flour
2 eggs
1 level tsp baking powder
2 level tbsp cocoa
2 tbsp hot water

Icing

50g/2ozs soft margarine
2 level tbsp golden syrup
3 level tbsp cocoa

Oven: Gas no. 3. 170°C. 325°F. Centre oven 35 minutes.
Cool in tin
Cake Tin: Line or grease a 7" square cake tin.

Method

1. Cream together margarine and sugar.
2. Gradually add beaten eggs.
3. Sieve flour, baking powder and cocoa.
4. Add to creamed mixture, fold in gently, then add the hot water, (should be smooth dropping consistency).
5. Put into prepared tin and bake. Cool in tin.
6. Icing: Put all ingredients in a saucepan, and heat gently till melted, and blended to a smooth mixture. Spread over cooled cake. When cold cut into squares.

Chocolate Fruit & Nut Treats

No Cooking

100g/4ozs plain chocolate – melted in bowl over hot water
125g/5oz pkt mixed fruit and nuts
100g/4ozs white chocolate – melted as above
75g/3ozs pkt tropical fruit mix (or dried apricots)

Lightly grease two baking trays

Method

1. Mix plain chocolate with fruit and nuts.
2. Mix white chocolate with tropical mix.
3. Place spoonfuls of each on baking trays.
4. Leave to set. (Keeps for a week).

Carob Fudge

No Cooking

50g/2ozs butter or margarine
25g/1oz Carob powder
50g/2ozs clear honey
25g/1oz soya flour
75g/3ozs ground almonds
1 tsp vanilla essence
25g/1oz chopped or ground almonds for coating

Method

1. Cream the butter and carob powder together until well mixed.
2. Add honey, soya flour, ground almonds and vanilla essence. Mix well.
3. Sprinkle the chopped almonds onto a clean surface, shape the carob mix into a roll, coat with nuts.

Keep in fridge, cut into 'bite' size pieces.

Kyrie Cake

150g/6ozs mixed dried fruit and peel
50g/1oz glacé cherries, chopped } *mixed together*
1 tsp lemon juice
1 Mars bar (and if available 1 chocolate liqueur or drop of sherry)
75g/3ozs margarine or butter
50g/2ozs brown sugar (soft)
2 eggs
100g/4ozs wholewheat plain flour
50g/1oz semolina
1 tsp baking powder

Oven: Gas no. 3. 325°F. 170°C. 40-45 minutes
7" cake tin greased.

Method

1. Cream together butter and sugar.
2. Add beaten eggs and flour, baking powder and semolina, with a drop of milk to give stiff consistency.
3. Add mixed fruit, lemon juice mixture.
4. Cut up Mars bar into small pieces and add to mixture.
5. Put into prepared tin and cook.

Serve warm, or cold with cream.

Flora Fridge Cake

no cooking

200g/8ozs dark chocolate
200g/8ozs butter
75g/3ozs icing sugar
2 eggs — lightly whisked
200g/8ozs chopped cherries, walnuts, raisins and angelica
2 pkts 'Nice' biscuits (200g/½lb size)
or plain semi sweet biscuits

Cake tin: Line a 1lb loaf tin with foil.

Method

1. Break up chocolate, put in pan with butter, melt gently together.
2. Gradually beat in the icing sugar, then add the eggs. Crush half the biscuits and stir into mixture with the chopped fruit and nuts.
3. Place 4 whole NICE biscuits in bottom of tin, cover with some of the mixture, then another 4 biscuits, continue layering until tin is full, finishing with biscuits.
4. Leave overnight in fridge, turn out onto plate. Cuts nicely into slices.

Chocolate Fondue

200g/8ozs plain chocolate
4 tbsp fresh orange juice
small can evaporated milk (chilled)
grated rind of ½ orange

Method

1. Melt chocolate with orange juice and 3 tbsp evaporated milk.
2. Whisk remaining evaporated milk until thickened, then fold into chocolate mixture (if wanting richer sauce, add few drops of rum).
3. Add grated orange rind. Keep warm.

Serve with pieces of fresh fruit or slices of chocolate cake.

Chocolate Cheesecake

Biscuit Base

200g/8ozs chocolate digestive biscuits
100g/4ozs butter

Filling

150g/6ozs Philadelphia cheese or other soft cheese
75g/3ozs caster sugar
25g/1oz cocoa powder
2 level tsp cornflour
2 eggs separated
150ml/¼ pint double cream
150g/6ozs fresh cherries (stoned) or other fruit

Icing sugar for sprinkling
Oven: Gas no. 4. 350°F. 180°C. 1 hour
Loose bottom cake tin.

Method

1. Crush biscuits using plastic bag and rolling pin, or food processor.
2. Melt butter in pan, stir in crushed biscuits.
3. Press this mixture over base, and up sides of greased tin - put to chill.
4. Beat cheese and sugar together until fluffy.
5. Beat in cocoa powder, cornflour, egg yolks and cream. Mix well.
6. Whisk egg whites until stiff, fold into mixture with metal spoon.
7. Add cherries or other fruit (if dried apricots, cut up, soak and cook first).
8. Pour into chilled base, put in oven, as above. When cooked, leave in tin to cool.
9. Chill overnight, decorate with icing sugar or chocolate flakes.

Chocolate Pots Serves 4 - 6

2 eggs, separated
25g/1oz sugar
100g/4ozs single cream
2 tsp finely ground coffee
100g/4ozs plain chocolate (melted)
1 tsp ground walnuts

Method

1. Whisk egg yolks and sugar in a bowl over a pan of just boiling water, until mixture is fluffy.
2. Remove from heat, but continue whisking until cool.
3. Stir the cream and coffee into melted chocolate.
4. Fold into the cool egg mixture.
5. Whisk egg whites, fold into the mixture, divide into individual pots, leave to set in fridge.
6. Decorate with double cream and walnuts.

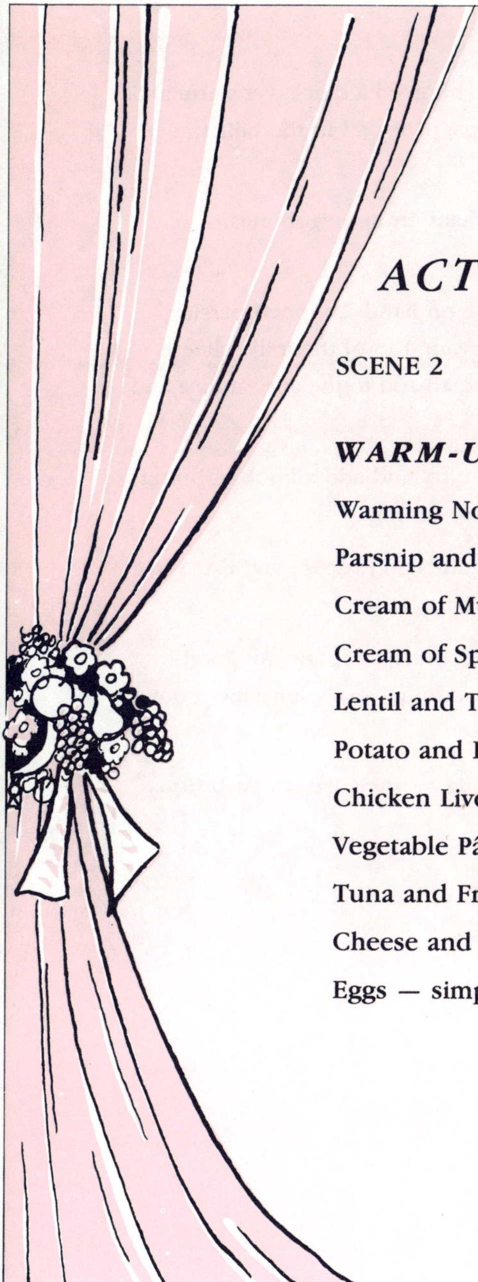

ACT 1

SCENE 2

WARM-UPS

WARM-UP NOTES

This speaks for itself, often you need a quick, yet warm and nourishing food. Soups, eggs, pâtés, all fit the bill, and these are just a few ideas.

Soups and stocks can be made from meat bones, vegetables or fish.

Garnishes should always be on hand: chopped parsley, mint, chives, cream, sour cream, top of the milk, cheese, slices of lemon or cucumber, all add to the appearance and the nourishment of soup.

Packet soups: If using these try and add a knob of butter, or beaten egg or grate cheese on top.

Pâtés: Also nourishing and quick to prepare and eat. Serve with hot toast or hot garlic bread.

Eggs: Boiled, poached, fried, omelettes, raw. All good instant 'Warm Ups', and providing 7% of your daily protein requirement.

Note: Other Cheese and Egg recipes are in 'Variations Part 1'.

Parsnip & Apple Soup

2 medium sized parsnips
1 cooking apple
570ml/1 pint vegetable stock
1 onion
570ml/1 pint milk
25g/1oz margarine
Pepper and salt and chopped parsley

Method

1. Chop parsnip, apple and onion into small pieces. Sauté in pan with margarine.
2. When soft, add stock and simmer for 30 minutes.
3. Remove from heat, add milk, seasoning and parsley.
4. Liquidise, re-heat and serve.

Nice with a swirl of fresh cream on top.

Cream of Mushroom Soup

100g/4ozs mushrooms, wiped and chopped
1 tbsp chopped parsley
280ml/½ pint vegetable stock
280ml/½ pint milk
25g/1oz butter
2 tbsp fresh cream
Ppper and salt to taste

Method

1. Place all ingredients, except cream, in a large saucepan.
2. Bring to the boil, simmer for 10 minutes.
3. Remove from heat, add cream and serve.

If a thicker soup is required, add a little flour and milk mixed to a paste, liquidise, then re-heat adding cream when you serve.

Cream of Spinach Soup

Serves 6

25g/1oz butter
1 large onion chopped
2 tbsp flour
2 pints chicken stock (stock cubes)
½ tsp grated nutmeg
1 tbsp lemon juice
600g/ 1½lb spinach chopped

Topping

50g/2ozs cream
chopped crispy bacon

Method

1. Melt butter in saucepan, add onion and fry until soft, not brown.
2. Sprinkle over the flour and cook while stirring (2 minutes).
3. Gradually add stock, nutmeg, pepper and salt, lemon juice and spinach, bring to the boil and simmer for approximately 20 minutes.
4. Blend the soup to a smooth purée, either by mashing, sieving or in a blender.
5. Return to pan and reheat.

Serve topped with cream and crispy bacon.

Lentil & Tomato Soup

100g/4ozs red lentils
2 tbsp vegetable oil
1 finely chopped onion
2 medium carrots (or parsnip) scrubbed and chopped
1 medium sized tin tomatoes (397g/14oz)
1 litre/1¾ pints vegetable stock
Salt and black pepper
1 tsp dried thyme
1 bay leaf

Method

1. Pick lentils over for stones (while still dry). Wash in sieve.
2. Heat oil in pan, fry onion and carrot until they begin to soften.
3. Add lentils, tomatoes, stock and herbs. Bring to the boil and simmer for 40-50 minutes.
4. Let it cool slightly, then sieve or liquidize.
5. Season to taste, re-heat and serve.

Potato & Leek Soup

400g/1lb leeks cleaned and chopped
1 small onion
25g/1oz butter
400g/1lb potatoes peeled and sliced
570ml/1pt chicken stock (or stock cube)
Salt and pepper
1 bay leaf

Topping

Sour or double cream
Watercress or chives

Method

1. Melt butter gently in saucepan, add leeks and onion, fry without browning 7 - 10 minutes.
2. Now add stock, potatoes, seasoning and bay leaf. Bring to boil, simmer for 20 minutes, take out bay leaf.
3. Remove from heat, rub through seive or put in blender.
4. Return to pan to heat.
5. Serve with a swirl of cream, watercress or chives on top.

Chicken Liver Pâté

Serves 5-6

400g/1lb chicken livers
200g/8ozs butter
1 finely chopped onion
2 tsp mustard powder
½ tsp grated nutmeg
Salt and black pepper
Extra 25g/1oz butter

Method

Cover livers with saltwater, bring to the boil and simmer for 20 minutes.
Drain, pat dry with kitchen tissue, put through fine mincer or liquidise.
Work the butter till it is soft.
Add onion, mustard, nutmeg and seasoning — then beat in the minced livers.
If a smooth texture required, put through a sieve.
Put pâté into an earthenware dish, run a little melted butter over the top and put in fridge to cool.
Serve with slices of lemon, and hot toast.

Vegetable Pâté Serves 4-6

125g/4ozs butter
1 onion finely chopped
1 clove garlic crushed
1 stick celery finely chopped
1 carrot finely chopped
225g/8ozs button mushrooms, chopped
Pepper and salt
1 tbsp lemon juice
2 tbsp flour
Small carton double cream (142ml/5 fl oz)

Method

1. Fry onion and garlic in butter over a low heat in frying pan for 5 - 6 minutes.
2. Toss the carrot and celery in the flour, and add to the pan, with seasoning and mushrooms.
3. Cook for 10 minutes, making sure the ingredients do not burn.
4. When cooked, remove from heat, cool, then add the lemon juice and fold in cream.
5. Put all in one dish, or individual dishes and put in fridge overnight.

Serve with garlic bread or toast.

Tuna & Fruit Pâté Serves 4

1 200g tin tuna in oil
25g/1oz butter, melted
1 eating apple, diced
25g/1oz chopped dried fruit
2 tsp lemon juice
1 tbsp mayonnaise
Salt and black pepper
Slices of lemon and parsley

Method

1. Pour butter over mashed tuna fish, mix well together.
2. Add seasoning, lemon juice and fruit — then mayonnaise. Mix well.
3. Put in dish, chill in fridge, garnish with lemon and parsley.

Serve with sticks of carrot, celery and bread.

Cheese & Walnut Pâté

200g/8oz cottage cheese
75g/3oz ground walnuts
50g/2oz butter
75g/3oz grated cheddar cheese
1 tsp ready made mustard
1 tsp caraway seeds
Salt and black pepper
4 tbsp fresh brown breadcrumbs

Method

1. Cream together butter and cottage cheese.
2. Mix in walnuts, cheese, caraway seeds and mustard. Season to taste, add breadcrumbs, stir all very well together.
3. Put into suitable container and leave overnight if possible in fridge, or for at least 3 hours so ingredients blend.

Serve at room temperature.

Eggs

Boiled (approximately 4 minutes) with buttered bread fingers.

Poached, on toast — add sliced tomatoes

Scrambled, on toast — add crispy bacon

Fried, with fried bread fingers

Omelette, variations: chopped herbs, sliced tomatoes, cheese, fried mushrooms, sweetcorn, cooked bacon.

Note: Other egg recipes in Variations, Part 1, on page 63.

ACT 1

SCENE 3

PRINCIPAL DISHES

Note Richer meat dishes are in the Entertaining chapter, page 167.

PRINCIPAL NOTICE BOARD

Dancers have spent years building their future, and building their bodies to do what is required of them.

BUILDING FOODS are those which contain the highest proportion of PROTEIN, the PRINCIPAL ones being MEAT, FISH, EGGS, MILK and CHEESE.

Beans, nuts, peas, lentils, oatmeal, wholemeal bread, brown rice and pasta are secondary protein foods.

Note: The body can only absorb enough proteins to replace the everyday wear and tear, little and often should be your motto as the wear and tear on a dancer's body is considerable — hence we hear the continual cry 'you must eat properly'.

Students should not be afraid to ask the butcher about various cuts of meat. Fresh meat, and sausages are best bought from a butcher, rather than supermarket. Have lean cuts where possible. Allow 100/150g (4 - 6oz) per person.

BEEF to	Roast: Sirloin, ribs, topside Grill: Fillet steak, rump steak, sirloin steak Braise or stew: Shin, skirt, chuck, mince
LAMB to	Roast: Leg, shoulder, breast Grill: Loin chops, chump chops, cutlets Stew: Best end of neck
PORK to	Roast: Leg, loin Grill or fry: Chops, tenderloin (escalopes)
VEAL	Escalopes or pie veal

Roasting Joints and Chicken

Beef cuts: 20 minutes per 400g/1lb. Temp: Gas no. 6. 400°F. 200°C.
Best not overdone.

Lamb cuts: 25 minutes per 400g/1lb. Temp: Gas no. 6. 400°F. 200°C.
I usually put into a hotter oven for first 15 minutes.

Pork cuts: 30 minutes per 400g/1lb. Temp: Gas no. 7. 425°F. 220°C.
Pork must not be undercooked. Ensure oven is really hot when you put the meat in, to seal and get the crackling crispy.

Chicken: If using a frozen one, make sure it is defrosted, preferably overnight in the fridge.
20 minutes per 400g/1lb plus 20 minutes extra.

Grilling

Chicken joints: 15 - 20 minutes

Lamb chops: 15 minutes, extra if liked crispy

Pork chops: 20 - 30 minutes, make sure well cooked.

Steaks, fillet, rump or sirloin: 3 minutes each side RARE. 6 minutes MEDIUM RARE. 10 minutes WELL DONE.

Sausages: 10 - 15 minutes.

Traditional Roast Dinner

Put joint (beef, lamb or pork) into a meat dish with dripping, oil or lard. Rub salt into skin, put into hot oven (times on previous page). An average joint is around 3lbs, so one can usually think in terms of 1 ½ hours cooking time. Baste the joint while cooking.

Apart from beef, which can safely be undercooked, cook meat well, better over than undercooked. If you haven't any dripping, spread lard, or vegetable oil over the joint.

Beef: serve Yorkshire puddings, Horseradish sauce or mustard.

Pork: serve apple sauce, or apricot sauce.

Lamb: serve mint sauce.

ROAST POTATOES

Put in saucepan with salted water. Bring to boil, simmer for about 10 minutes. Drain water off.

In the meantime, heat dripping in meat pan, when hot put potatoes into fat (gently, don't splash) and return to hot oven for about 30/40 minutes. Once again, to get crispy potatoes one needs a hot oven, Gas no. 6, 400°F. 200°C. If there is room round your joint, put the potatoes round it, usually about half way through the cooking time. When you take the meat out, and while you are carving, you can turn the oven even higher to crisp the potatoes.

YORKSHIRE PUDDINGS

100g/4ozs plain flour
¼ tsp salt
1 egg
280mls/½ pint milk
Dripping — about 25g/1oz

Method

1. Sieve flour and salt into a bowl. Make a well in the centre, add the egg, and enough milk to make a smooth batter. Mix well, add rest of milk and a drop of water if too thick. Beat well with whisk, or electric mixer — this allows air in and makes puddings lighter.
2. Melt fat in baking tin, or small cake tins if making individual puddings (about ½ tsp in each tin).
3. Put tin in oven for few minutes till piping hot, then pour the batter into big tin, or small tins.
4. Back in oven 30/40 minutes, till well risen and brown.
5.(Small puddings sometimes take less time 20/30 minutes).

GRAVY

When meat is taken from meat tin, use the juices to mix the gravy in. This makes all the difference to the flavour of the dinner. Do not make gravy very thick for a roast dinner.

Cottage Pie Serves 4

400g/1lb minced beef
1 medium onion, sliced
Seasoning and mixed herbs
25g/1oz dripping
300ml/approximately ½ pint stock (use vegetable cube or Oxo)
1 tbsp flour
½ tsp Worcester sauce
400g/1lb potatoes

Oven: Gas no. 7. 425°F. 220°C.
2 pint casserole dish

Method

1. Melt dripping in saucepan, add onion and fry gently. Add mince and stir until the meat begins to brown, about 5 minutes.
2. Pour in stock, seasoning and sprinkle of herbs. Put on lid and simmer gently for 20 - 25 minutes.
3. Remove from heat. Mix the flour with a little water, add to the meat, stirring well. Also add the Worcester sauce. Put into casserole dish.
4. Boil the potatoes, mash with milk and butter. Put on top of mince, spread with a fork.
5. Put in oven until brown on top, about 20 - 25 minutes. Sprinkle chopped parsley on before serving.

If preferred, you can slice parboiled potatoes on top of mince, instead of mashed potatoes.

Basic Mince Serves 4

400g/1lb minced beef
Seasoning
1 medium onion
25g/1oz dripping
Stock and flour (as for Cottage Pie)
Worcester sauce

Method

Cook as for Cottage Pie.
Mince is lovely with rice or potatoes and vegetables or used in savoury pancakes.
A variety of tastes can be achieved by adding during the last 10 minutes of cooking: chopped mushrooms, curry powder, tomato purée, chopped pepper, garlic or whatever flavour you fancy.

Chops & Steak

LAMB CHOPS

Trim away fat and skin, so that the chop looks appetizing.

Season on each side with pepper and salt.

Grill or fry, making sure you put under preheated hot grill or hot pan for a few moments, each side, then lower heat, and cook according to the table on page 202.

Serve with new potatoes and fresh vegetables, or side salad and french bread.

Don't forget the mint sauce.

PORK CHOPS

Trim excess fat, season, grill under preheated hot grill each side for 5 minutes then turn down heat and cook for further 20 minutes.

Serve with potatoes, vegetables and apple sauce or garnish with slices of orange and chopped parsley, baked potato in jacket and salad.

FILLET OR RUMP STEAK

Have grill or pan hot.

Put steaks on a plate, sprinkle with pepper and salt, crushed garlic (if liked), a dash of Worcester sauce and a knob of butter, both sides of steaks.

Put under grill, or in pan. Cook according to table of cooking times for rare, medium or well done.

Last few minutes, pour a drop of red wine over the steaks, return to heat.

Serve immediately on to hot plates, pour juices over, garnish with parsley.

Serve with new or sauté potatoes, side salad or fresh vegetables.

Steak à la Crème

1 or 2 steaks, rump or fillet
100g/4oz mushrooms
Knob of butter
1 tbsp brandy
4 tbsp single cream
Salt & black pepper
Parsley to trim

Method

1. Heat butter in heavy pan until just turning brown, turn heat down a little, put steaks into pan, sprinkle with salt and pepper, turn after 2 - 3 minutes to other side and cook for further 2 - 3 minutes.
2. Remove from pan, put to keep warm. (Cook longer if well-done steak is required).
3. Chop mushrooms, add to juices in pan and cook until soft. Add brandy, return steaks to pan, pour on half the cream, cook gently for 3 - 4 minutes, add rest of cream.

Serve at once sprinkled with parsley.

Liver & Bacon Serves 3 or 4

200g/½lb lamb's or calves liver — thinly cut
Rasher of bacon for each person
Dripping or butter about 25g/1oz
Seasoned flour
2 tbsp lemon juice or milk (milk takes away the strong flavour)

Method

1. Sprinkle liver slices with lemon juice, or lay them in milk for 5 minutes. Remove, pat dry with paper towel, coat slices in seasoned flour.
2. Melt dripping in frying pan. When hot, put bacon slices in, cook both sides, remove and put to keep warm.
3. Now put liver slices into fat. Cook 5 - 6 minutes each side, until tender.
4. Put with bacon, use the remaining juices in the pan to make the gravy. Does not usually need any more thickening or browning, just vegetable stock or water.
5. Arrange liver and bacon on serving dish, garnish with parsley and lemon wedges if liked, or fry till soft one large sliced onion, and put on serving dish with liver and bacon.

For variety when cooking liver you can sprinkle mixed herbs on to the liver while it is cooking, or crush a garlic clove and add to the liver.

Basic Beef Casserole Serves 4

400g/1lb stewing steak
Seasoned flour
Medium onion, sliced
Dried mixed herbs (about 1 tsp)
280ml/½ pint stock, or water and 2 Oxo cubes
Dripping or butter

Oven: Gas no. 6. 400°F. 200°C. for first 20 minutes, then lower to Gas no. 3. 325°F. 170°C. for at least 2½ hours until meat is tender. Add more seasoning if required.

Method

1. Cut meat into 2cm/1″ pieces, trimming away fat and gristle. Coat in seasoned flour.
2. Melt dripping or butter in saucepan, sauté the sliced onion. Remove onion and put to one side, add the flavoured meat, stir until most of the meat is sealed and slightly brown.
3. Sprinkle on herbs, add stock and mix well, return onion to pan.
4. Transfer to casserole with a lid. (1.25 litre/2 pint size).
5. Put in oven, cook as instructions above.

Grandma's lamb stew

Grandma's Lamb Stew Serves 4 - 6

This is best cooked the day before, put in fridge so that when cold, the fat can be taken off. This is a very inexpensive, very nourishing meal, and so tasty.

1kg/2¼lbs Best end of neck (stewing lamb)
1 medium onion
400g/1lb carrots
400g/1lb potatoes
200g/½lb fresh or frozen peas
Worcester sauce
2 stock cubes
1 tsp mixed herbs
Salt and black pepper

Method

1. Put meat into saucepan with salt, cover with water. Bring to the boil, removing scum as it appears. Turn heat down and leave to simmer for ¾ hour.
2. Take meat out, put onto plate, strain stock into a jug, let both cool then put in fridge.

Next day

3. Chop up and cook carrots, onion and potatoes together for 20 minutes. While cooking take meat, remove fat layer on top of stock and any from meat.
4. Remove meat pieces from bones, discarding gristle and fat.
5. Put stock and meat into vegetables (do not drain away water vegetables have been cooking in) add herbs, Worcester sauce, stock cubes, seasoning.
6. Simmer for ½ hour, add peas during the last 5 minutes. This is a complete meal.

Chicken à la Flora Serves 3 or 4

3 or 4 breasts of chicken, skinned and boned
280mls/½ pint milk (or single cream if special occasion)
2 tbsp white wine
50g/2oz butter and 1 tbsp vegetable oil
100g/½lb mushrooms
Small tin chicken liver pâté (optional)
Seasoned flour
Salt and black pepper
½ tsp tarragon
½ tsp sweet basil

Method

1. If I have bought chicken on the bone, I remove the chicken half way through cooking, and when cool, remove the flesh from the bone, and discard skin. Return to pan and carry on cooking. Marks & Spencer skinned chicken breasts are ideal for this dish.
2. Wash and pat dry chicken pieces, coat in seasoned flour.
3. Melt butter and oil in large shallow pan, add chicken breasts and brown slightly on both sides. Turn down heat, pour over the milk (or cream) and bring to boil, then simmer covered for 20 mins.
4. Now add mushrooms, seasoning, basil, tarragon and, if using — the pâté.
5. Put lid on, and simmer gently for 5 - 6 minutes (do not let stick to bottom of pan). At last moment add some extra cream, or top of the milk, and chopped parsley.

Serve on bed of rice, with side salad or sauté potatoes and fresh vegetables.

Lemon Sauce Chicken Serves 4

1 3lb chicken (1½kg)
100g/4oz butter
Juice of one lemon, 1 lemon cut in quarters
¼ tsp tarragon
Salt and black pepper

Sauce

50g/2oz butter
1 tbsp flour
140ml/

Oven: Gas no. 6. 400°F. 200°C.

Method

1. Wash and wipe dry the chicken.
2. Mix together 100g butter with juice of lemon, salt and pepper to taste, add tarragon and spread thickly over breast of chicken.
3. Put lemon quarters inside chicken, put chicken into roasting tin, cover with foil, put into oven and cook for 1½ to 1¾ hours, basting frequently. Remove foil for last ½ hour.
4. Make sauce by melting butter in small saucepan. Blend in flour, gradually stir in stock and lemon juice, to make a smooth sauce.
5. Simmer 2 - 3 minutes. Add cream at the last moment.
6. Place chicken on bed of rice, pour cream sauce over chicken, decorate with lemon slices.

Grilled Chicken with Almonds
Serves 4

4 chicken pieces
Butter or oil
Seasoning
100g/4ozs blanched almonds

Method

1. Wipe clean the chicken, rub salt and pepper into skin, then brush with oil or butter.
2. Place on grill pan, put under preheated hot grill, turning regularly for 20 - 25 minutes until well cooked.
3. When cooked put on serving plate, drain any juices into a small pan, add knob of butter, put almonds in and brown over heat 5 - 7 minutes.
4. Top chicken pieces with the almonds.

Serve with sauté potatoes and salad.

Pork or Veal Escalopes in Orange

Serves 4

4 escalopes of veal or pork
2 tbsp seasoned flour
50g/2oz dripping
1 tbsp brown sugar
½ tbsp ground ginger
Grated rind and juice of 2 oranges
Orange segments for garnish
2 tbsp cream or top of milk

Method

1. Coat escalopes with seasoned flour. Melt dripping in pan, until hot, put in meat, brown slightly on both sides. Remove and leave to keep warm.
2. Stir any remaining flour, together with sugar, ginger, orange rind and juice into pan, mix together, return meat to pan in the sauce, cover with lid, cook gently for 20 - 30 minutes.
3. Add cream at last moment.

Serve on bed of rice, garnished with orange segments.

American Meat Loaf

Serves 4 - 5

400g/1lb mince
1 egg, lightly beaten
200g/½lb soft brown breadcrumbs
1 small onion, chopped
Little stock, or dissolved Oxo
Dash of Worcester sauce
Salt and pepper
Tomato ketchup

Oven: Gas no. 5. 375°F. 190°C.
Tin: 400g/1lb loaf tin, greased.

Method

1. Put all ingredients into a bowl. Mix well.
2. Put into a greased 400g/1lb loaf tin, cover with foil.
3. Bake in moderate oven for 1 hour. Turn out, upside down on a dish when cooked, spread top with tomato ketchup, thickly sprinkle with parsley.

Serve hot with salad or vegetables.

Gammon & Pineapple

4 gammon steaks
Tin pineapple rings

Method

1. Heat grill fairly hot.
2. Snip round edges of gammons to stop them curling, remove any rind.
3. Place under grill for 5 minutes each side.

Serve with pineapple rings on top.

Apricot & Lamb Pie

200g/8oz cold, cooked lamb (this is an ideal way to use up cold lamb from a roast)
50g/2oz dried apricots
1 pepper, deseeded
1 pkt (small) frozen pastry (or make own puff pastry)
25g/1oz flour
25g/1oz butter
Seasoning and tsp lemon juice
50g/2oz of fresh orange juice, or juice of 2 oranges
Oven: Gas no. 6. 400°F. 200°C.
1 pint pie dish

Method

1. Chop up the cold lamb into 2cm/1″ pieces, soak apricots overnight, or cook for 20 minutes, then cut up.
2. Chop pepper into small pieces.
3. Put meat, apricots and pepper into a pan with the orange juice, simmer gently for 15 minutes.
4. Add flour and butter mixed together, stir gently until well blended, add seasoning. Put mixture into a pie dish.
5. Roll out pastry 5mm/¼″ thick, cover meat.
Bake in oven 10 - 15 minutes.

Stir-Fry Chicken & Pepper Curry

by David

2 chicken breasts - chopped in pieces
1 egg white
1 red & 1 green pepper or 2 carrots
140mls/¼pt chicken stock
1 tbsp light soy sauce
1 tbsp dry sherry
2 tsp Madras curry powder
½ tsp salt
1 tsp cornflour
1 - 2 tbsp ground nut oil

Method

1. Coat chicken pieces with egg white and salt. Leave in fridge for approx ½ hour.
2. Heat oil in wok or heavy pan until oil begins to smoke, put chicken pieces in, stir fry for 2 minutes, (finished when white) remove from pan.
3. Stir fry peppers or carrots for 2 minutes, add chicken stir fry a further 2 minutes.
4. Add soy sauce, sherry, curry powder, salt and cornflour to pan, stir 1 minute until well blended.

Serve with brown rice.

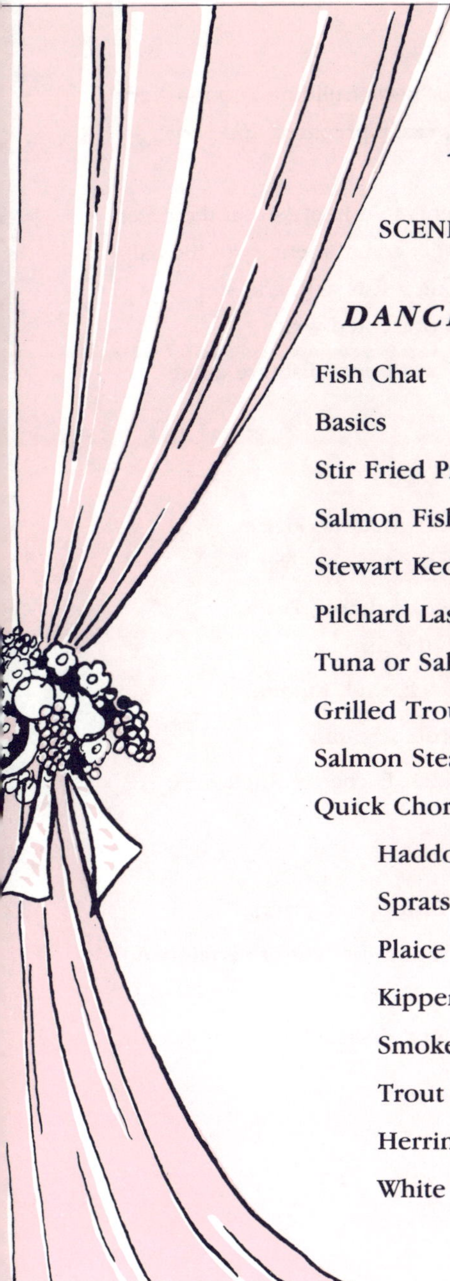

ACT 1

SCENE 4

DANCING WITH SOUL!

FISH CHAT

Here we have a very important Body Building Food — Very often neglected, but so tasty, easily prepared and very nourishing.

I have heard Boy Ballet Students told in class that their feet look like DEAD FISH — not very complimentary to the fish, for they look most attractive on a fish stall, and so appetizing when cooked and presented well.

Buy fresh if possible. Frozen and tinned fish are good alternatives.

TYPES

White Fish i.e. Cod, Hake, Sole, Halibut, Plaice
The fat and oil being concentrated in the liver.

Oily Fish i.e. Herring, Mackerel, Salmon, Trout
The fat is distributed through the fish.

Smoked Fish: Salmon, Haddock, Cod, Kippers

Shell Fish: Prawns, Crab, Lobster, Scampi

Tinned: Tuna, Salmon, Sardines, Pilchards, Anchovies, Mackerel, Herrings.

And of course,

Cockles, Mussels, Winkles, Scallops, Oysters.

Fish should be used on the day it is bought or certainly no later than the next day.

FISHMONGERS will willingly gut, de-head and fillet fish for you if you ask.

BASICS

BAKED, GRILLED, POACHED, FRIED, FISH PIES ETC.

BAKING Wrap cleaned fish in foil, adding butter and seasoning, or lemon juice. Cook at approx. Gas no. 5. 375°F. 190°C., for 20 - 30 minutes. Can also be put into ovenproof dish, covered with foil and baked.

POACHING This means cooking the fish in liquid, either milk, water, fish stock or of course wine. Cook gently over low heat, flavour liquid with a bay leaf and seasoning, approx 15 - 20 minutes depending on size of fish, obviously 1 portion would only take 7 - 10 minutes.

FRYING Dry fish well, coat in seasoned flour, or egg and breadcrumbs, or dip in batter. Fry quickly in hot fat or oil, a few minutes each side, drain on kitchen paper.

GRILLING Make sure grill is hot first. Dry fish well, put on grill pan (lined with foil if preferred) dot with butter. Whole fish need grilling both sides, approx 5 - 7 minutes each side. Fillets or flat fish only need grilling one side.

SAUCES to serve with fish in DRESSING UP section on page 133.

Stir Fried Prawns with Broccoli

200g/8oz shelled prawns
100g/4oz broccoli spears (or courgettes or cauliflower)
2 tbsp dry white wine
1 egg white
1 tbsp cornflour
1 tbsp sherry
2 tbsp soy sauce
1 tsp sesame oil
1 clove garlic, crushed
2 tbsp ground nut oil
½ tsp ground ginger

Method

1. Blanch broccoli (or courgettes or cauliflower) in boiling water for 1 - 2 minutes, drain well.
2. Blend cornflour with white wine and egg white, put prawns into this.
3. Put oil into wok or heavy pan, get it really hot, stir fry prawns 1 - 2 minutes until changed colour. Add sherry, soy sauce, sesame oil, stirring continually. Add crushed garlic and ginger, then broccoli spears, fry for 1 - 2 minutes stirring continually.

Serve immediately on a bed of brown rice.

Salmon Fish Cakes Serves 3 - 4

1 can red salmon (213g/7½oz)
1lb potatoes, boiled and mashed
Pepper and salt
Dash of worcestershire sauce
Chopped parsley
Lemon wedges
Seasoned flour

Method

1. Drain liquid from salmon, put salmon in basin, remove skin and small pieces of bone, mash well.
2. Now add the mashed potato to the salmon,(if you want stronger salmon taste, add little less potato); add seasoning, sprinkling of parsley and Worcestershire Sauce.
3. Put seasoned flour onto plate, mould the salmon mixture into fishcake size pieces, and shape, coat in flour.
4. Melt lard or dripping in frying pan. When nice and hot put fish cakes in, fry for 6 - 7 minutes each side until brown.

Serve garnished with lemon wedges, nice hot or cold.

Stewart's Kedgeree

Serves 4 - 6

600g/1½lbs smoked haddock
75g/3oz butter
4 hardboiled eggs
3 tbsp chopped parsley
1 tbsp lemon juice
Salt and black pepper
200g/8oz long grain rice

Method

1. Place haddock in saucepan, cover with cold water, bring to boil, put lid on and simmer for 10 minutes.
2. Drain off liquid into a jug and set aside.
3. Put cooked fish on to a plate, remove any small bones and skin, flake fish, then leave somewhere to keep warm.
4. Hardboil the eggs, set aside.
5. Cook rice in 570ml/1pt of the fish liquid for 15 - 20 minutes until soft.
6. When rice has absorbed all liquid and is cooked add to it the flaked fish, butter, 3 chopped hardboiled eggs, parsley, lemon juice and salt and pepper.
7. Warm all through in the oven, or in a saucepan.
8. Transfer to a dish, garnish with the other hard boiled egg cut into quarters, sprinkle with parsley.

A meal on its own.

Pilchard Lasagne Serves 4 - 5

200g/8oz lasagne verdi
1 tbsp cooking oil
50g/2oz margarine or butter
1 onion chopped
1 tin tomatoes (213g/7½ozs) - juice drained off
1 tin pilchards (400g/12 - 14ozs in tomato sauce)
1 tsp dried oregano
Salt and pepper
25g/1oz flour
280ml/½ pt milk
75g/3oz grated cheddar cheese
pinch of nutmeg

Oven: Gas No. 5. 375°F. 190°C.
Ovenproof shallow dish

Method

1. Cook lasagne in boiling salted water for 15 minutes. You can also buy ready cooked lasagne.
2. Drain, and put into colander, run under cold water, then put on cloth to dry.
3. Heat oil, and 25g/1oz of margarine in a pan, add onion and cook until soft, add tomatoes, pilchards and oregano and seasoning, gently mix with wooden spoon. Keep warm.
4. Place flour, remaining margarine and milk into a pan, mix to a smooth paste, cook gently. When thick add cheese, seasoning and nutmeg.
5. Grease a shallow ovenproof dish, arrange alternate layers of lasagne, fish mixture, and cheese sauce in dish, finishing with cheese sauce. Sprinkle a little extra cheese on top. Cook in oven for 30 minutes.

Garnish with tomato slices and parsley.

Tuna or Salmon Slice Serves 4

Tuna fish is noted for being the main standby diet when on tour! But this slice bears no resemblance to just Tuna.

1 tin 213g/7 ½oz Tuna fish (or you can use tinned salmon)
2 hard boiled eggs — chopped
50g/2oz butter — melted
2 tbsp chopped parsley
1 tbsp chopped chives (or small onion if no chives)
salt and pepper
2 tbsp tomato ketchup
50g/2oz cooked rice
350g/13oz pkt frozen puff pastry (or make own pastry)

Oven: Preheated to Gas No. 7. 425°F. 220°C.
Baking Tray

Method

1. Place tuna fish (drained) into a basin, with the cooked rice, chopped eggs, parsley, chives, tomato ketchup, seasoning and melted butter, fold all together until well mixed but not mashed.
2. Roll out pastry on floured surface (35cm/14″ x 25cm/10″).
3. Place fish mixture onto the pastry, bring up sides and fold over on top.
4. Seal by dampening pastry edges with water, then seal ends in the same manner.
5. Pick up the pastry and put onto baking tray with the sealed part at the bottom. Brush top with beaten egg and bake for 30 - 40 minutes until brown.

Serve hot or cold, with salad.

You might find it easier to put this filling in when the pastry is already on the baking tray, as it is a little difficult to pick up.

Grilled Trout with Almonds

4 trout medium size (adjust ingredients if only 1 or 2 trout)
100g/4oz butter
2 tbsp lemon juice
Salt and pepper
100g/4oz slivered almonds
50g/2oz butter
lemon wedges and parsley sprigs

Method

1. Rub fish, (after gutting, de-scaling and cleaning well, then patting dry) with butter on each side, sprinkle with salt and pepper, pour over lemon juice and put under the preheated grill (fairly hot) and cook 6 - 8 minutes each side. You can usually tell if they are cooked by putting a pointed knife through the thickest part of the fish, it will easily go into the fish if cooked.
2. Remove and put on to serving dish and keep warm.
3. Put remaining butter and almonds into the grill pan, and put under hot grill until brown and crispy — take care as it burns very quickly.
4. Sprinkle over the fish, pour remaining juices over fish, and garnish with lemon and parsley.

Serve with potatoes and vegetables.

Salmon Steaks with Sour Cream

2 salmon steaks about 2.5cm/1" thick
25g/1oz butter
1 tbsp lemon juice
1 carton soured cream
Chopped parsley
Salt and pepper

Method

1. Rinse and dry the steaks, put into ovenproof shallow dish, put half the butter on top, put under moderate grill for 4 - 5 minutes.
2. Turn steaks, put rest of butter on then return to grill to cook other side 4 - 5 minutes, until fish is golden colour. Transfer to serving dish.
3. Stir the soured cream, lemon juice, parsley, salt and black pepper into remaining juices and pour over the salmon steaks.

Serve with a lemon twist.

QUICK CHORUS LINE

HADDOCK smoked, is lovely just poached in water approx. 10 minutes. Lift out, drain and serve with knob of butter or poached egg on top.

SPRATS When frying or grilling these, they must be done quickly in hot fat, or under hot grill. Dip in flour after washing and drying (leave heads & tails on) fry 2 -3 minutes each side. Drain on kitchen paper and serve with lemon slices.

KIPPERS smoked, grill or fry for 5 - 6 minutes. Serve with knob of butter and brown bread.

SMOKED SALMON Serve with lemon slices, black pepper, thin brown bread and butter — no cooking.

TROUT or MACKEREL gutted, washed, dried. Coat in flour, wrap in foil with piece of butter, put in oven Gas No. 5. 375°F. 190°C. for 20 - 30 minutes. Nice served with gooseberry or apricot sauce.

HERRINGS Take off heads, gut, wash and dry. Dip in flour, season, fry in hot fat, or grill for approx 6 - 10 minutes, serve with horseradish sauce.

WHITE FISH Cod, Sole, Plaice, etc. Wash, pat dry. Poach in seasoned milk or white wine for 7 - 10 minutes, drain, serve garnished with lemon slices or parsley, or dip in seasoned flour, fry in shallow pan with little oil or butter, turn carefully. 7 - 8 minutes. Serve with creamed potatoes or chips, lemon slices, watercress.

FISH & CHIPS nearest fish & chip shop!

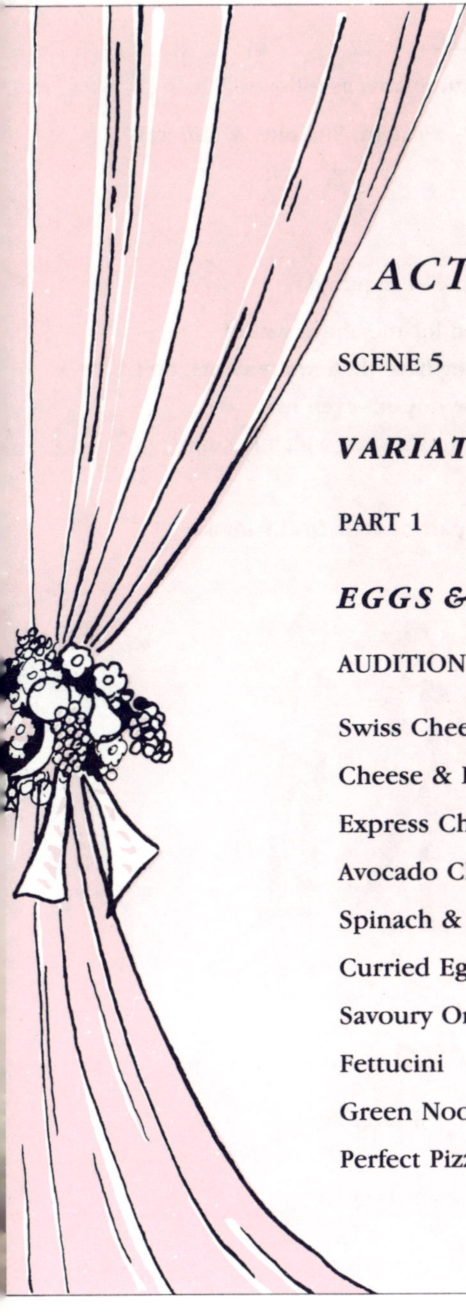

ACT 1

SCENE 5

VARIATIONS PARTS 1, 2 & 3

PART 1

EGGS & CHEESE

AUDITION NOTICE

2 vacancies to be filled, requirements as follows:

1. Body Building Qualities — Protein, Vitamins & Minerals
2. Versatility
3. Easy Preparation
4. Availability at any Time
5. Ability to become 'Principal' if required

EGGS & CHEESE auditioned for the above would obviously get the job, for they have the requirements, and are also very tolerant. cheese doesn't even have to be young, MATURE adds to its desirability, which is quite something these days!

These two foods should be part of your DAILY intake.

A bunch of lemons

Swiss Cheese Pie Serves 4

100g/4oz shortcrust pastry
100g/4oz swiss cheese, grated
1 tbsp plain flour
3 large eggs
140ml/¼ pint single cream
Seasoning

Oven: Gas no. 4. 350°F. 180°C.
8" flan tin or ring

Method

1. Roll out pastry to fit tin, press in and up sides put on a baking tray — set aside to chill.
2. In a bowl mix together grated cheese, flour, seasoning and sprinkle over pastry, lightly beat egg and cream, pour over cheese mixture.
3. Bake for 30 - 40 minutes — should be well risen.

Serve with tossed green salad.

Cheese & Leek Natasha

Base

150g/6oz breadcrumbs
50g/2oz butter
100g/4oz Cheddar cheese, grated
100g/4oz chopped mixed nuts
½ tsp mixed herbs
1 clove garlic, crushed

Oven: Gas no. 7. 425°F. 220°C.
11" x 7" tin

Sauce

3 leeks
4 tomatoes
50g/2oz butter
25g/2oz flour
280ml/½ pint milk
4 tbsp breadcrumbs
Salt & black pepper

Method:

Base:

1. Mix butter with breadcrumbs, add rest of base ingredients, mix well, press into tin.

Sauce:

2. Slice leeks, chop tomatoes, melt butter in pan. Sauté leeks for 5 minutes.
3. Stir in flour, add milk stirring constantly bring to boil. Add rest of ingredients, except breadcrumbs, and simmer for 5 minutes until tomato is soft.
4. Spoon mixture over base, sprinkle with breadcrumbs, put in oven and bake for 20 minutes.

Express Cheese Supper

100g/4oz grated Cheddar cheese
2 eggs
100g/4oz breadcrumbs
1 tsp french mustard
280ml/ ½ pint milk
Top of milk
Chopped parsley
Pepper & Salt
1 chopped onion

Oven: Gas no. 6. 400°F. 200°C.
Shallow ovenproof dish

Method

1. Peel & chop onion, put all ingredients into liquidizer, blend until smooth.
2. Pour into a greased shallow ovenproof dish, bake approx. 35 minutes.

Avocado Cheese

1 or 2 ripe avocado pears
Juice of 1 lemon
200g/8oz cottage or cream cheese
1 small onion & stick of celery
1 eating apple
pepper & salt

Method

1. Cut avocado in half, take out stone, spoon out flesh and mash with lemon juice.
2. Combine this with the cottage or cream cheese.
3. Chop the onion, celery and apple up, add to the mixture, with seasoning, return the cheese and avocado mixture to the avocado skins.

Serve on a bed of lettuce, garnished with lemon.

Spinach & Cheese Pancakes

Pancake batter

100g/4oz plain flour
1 egg
½ tsp salt
280ml/½ pint milk
Butter or oil for frying

Filling

600g/1½lb spinach or 200g/8oz frozen spinach
50g/2oz butter
Salt & pepper
100g/4oz flour
140ml/5oz single cream
50g/2oz strong cheese or Stilton
280ml/ ½ pint milk

Oven: Gas no. 4. 350°F. 180°C.
Shallow ovenproof dish

Method

Pancakes

1. Sift flour & salt, add egg, beat, gradually add milk, whisk well.
2. Heat butter in small fry pan until VERY hot, pour in enough batter to coat the bottom, cook until pancake begins to curl at edges, flip over with a slice, or toss, fry other side.
3. Turn onto a warm plate, put to keep warm, continue until all the pancakes are cooked, makes 7 - 8.

Filling

4. Wash spinach, cook for a few minutes until tender, drain well and chop.
5. Heat butter (1oz) in pan, add spinach, pepper and salt, now put in half the flour (2oz) and fresh cream, cook for a few minutes.
6. Divide this mixture between the pancakes, folding each over, and then putting into a shallow oven-proof dish.
7. Melt remaining butter in a pan, stir in remaining flour, gradually add milk stirring constantly until sauce thickens and there are no lumps, stir in cheese and seasoning.
8. Pour sauce over pancakes, cover with foil and put into oven. Bake for 20 - 30 minutes.

Curried Eggs

4 hardboiled eggs
25g/1oz butter
1 tsp curry powder
25g/1oz flour
280ml/½ pint milk
50g/2oz sultanas
1 eating apple, chopped
Pepper & salt

Method

1. Cut eggs in half longways, put them yolk side down in serving dish.
2. Melt butter in pan, stir in flour & curry powder, add chopped apple and milk, bring to boil, cook until sauce thickens.
3. Stir in the sultanas and pepper and salt, pour this over the eggs.

Serve with boiled rice.

Savoury Omelette

Fillings listed below

2 eggs (per person)
Salt & black pepper
15g/½oz butter

Method

1. Beat eggs with seasoning, melt butter in pan (20cm/8″). When fat is sizzling, add eggs.
2. As edges start to cook, draw mixture to centre with a fork to enable egg to flow underneath.
3. When nearly cooked add mixture on half of the omelette, fold over, when sealed remove on to a warmed plate, sprinkle with parsley.

Suggested fillings:

25g/1oz grated Cheddar cheese
25g/1oz sliced Stilton cheese
50g/2oz mushrooms & beansprouts (sautéed in butter for 3 minutes).
50g/2oz sweetcorn (tinned or cooked)
50g/2oz chopped ham or bacon (cooked ham, crispy bacon)
25g/1oz chopped chives & lettuce

Fettucini

150g/6oz fettucini or tagliatelle
25g/1oz butter
4 tbsp double cream
50g/2oz parmesan cheese
1 tbsp sherry
Salt & black pepper

Method

1. Bring salted water to boil in large saucepan, add pasta (fettucini or tagliatelle), stir until it boils, cook 3 - 5 minutes, drain into colander.
2. Melt butter in frying pan. When hot add the pasta, toss in the butter, then add the sherry, seasoning, cream and parmesan.
3. Toss well — turn on the warm plate or dish, sprinkle with parsley.

Serve with green salad, chunks brown bread.

Green Noodles with Cheese & Cream

400g/1lb green noodles (tagliatelle)
280ml/½ pint single cream
50g/2oz grated soft cheese (or use cream cheese)
50g/2oz butter
Parmesan cheese
Salt & black pepper

Method

1. Cook noodles in plenty of boiling salt water until tender, drain in colander, rinse under cold tap.
2. Put butter into large pan, together with cream and

cheese, heat GENTLY until all combined.

3. Add the drained noodles, re-heat, serve at once in dish, sprinkled with parmesan cheese.

Lovely with green salad and brown bread.

Perfect Pizza

This amount makes 2 - 3 pizzas

Base

200g/8oz white flour
200g/8oz brown flour
25g/½oz fresh yeast (or dried yeast)
10oz/ ½ pint milk
1 tsp salt
25g/½oz butter or margarine

Filling:

2 medium onions
1 tbsp cooking oil
600g/1½lb tomatoes (or tinned)
1 clove garlic
Salt & black pepper
2 tsp dried basil

Topping:

150g/6oz grated cheese
100g/4oz chopped mushrooms

Oven: Gas no. 5. 375°F. 180°C.

Method

Bases:

1. Soften the yeast with a little of the milk.
2. Heat half the milk with the butter, when melted pour into remaining cold milk.
3. Put flours into warmed bowl, add salt, make a well in centre, add yeast and warmed milk & butter mix, leave to 'sponge' for 20 minutes. Knead until smooth (on floured board).
4. Divide dough into 2 or 3 depending on size of pizza required, shape into rounds by kneading, stretching etc., pull & push it into about 9″ dia. rounds. Put onto lightly greased baking trays — brush all over with oil.

Tomato mix fillings:

5. Peel, slice onions finely, sauté gently in oil in pan, skin & slice tomatoes, add to onion (use juice as well if using tinned tomatoes). Cook until thick pulp — add dried herbs, crushed garlic, salt & pepper and put to cool.
6. Divide tomato mixture between pizza bases, reserve some of the juices to pour over pizzas when cooked (makes then moister).
7. Top with cheese and mushrooms (or salami, or anchovies depending on your taste. I always add extra cheese).
8. Bake on middle shelf of oven, 25 - 35 minutes. During last 10 minutes of cooking, if pizzas look dry I add a little more tomato juice, little more cheese, return to oven for 5 minutes.

Tip

When removed from oven, if edges of pastry look dry, moisten them with a little water whilst still hot.

PART 2

VEGETABLES & SALADS

PROTECTIVE foods, containing most vitamins and minerals VEGETABLES, SALADS & FRUIT must be eaten EVERY day.

A choreographer would, I'm sure, create a wonderful contemporary dance from these foods, think of the variety in colour, shape and size, the best are very young, and they are of course readily available, just imagine —

'Salad Suite' or 'Fruit Facade'!

They are yours for growing or buying, then eating — RAW whenever possible. Vegetables should have as little cooking as possible preferably steamed or blanched (or microwaved). Undercook if you are in doubt.

ROOT VEGETABLES such as carrots, swedes and parsnips are best cut into slices, chopped or grated. Steamed, boiled or stir fried for 5 - 10 minutes, obviously one must use ones own judgement on this.

POTATOES are indeed obliging, and don't mind being boiled, with or without skins, roast in the oven, baked in Jackets, sauté in butter, chipped, or made into croquettes.

GREEN VEGETABLES such as broccoli, sprouts, calabrese, cauliflower and kale are best steamed or put into boiling salted water for 5 - 7 minutes, drained in colander, rinsed under cold water, then returned to be reheated just before serving. This preserves the colour and firmness. Spinach needs no added water, it cooks in what is left after washing, and needs only 4 - 5 minutes cooking.

Mushrooms in Soured Cream

3 tbsp butter or margarine
1 medium onion, finely chopped
400g/1lb mushrooms, sliced
1 small carton soured cream
Pepper & salt
Chopped parsley to garnish

Method

1. In large pan melt butter, sauté onion until soft, add sliced mushrooms, sauté approx. 4 - 5 minutes stirring frequently.
2. Remove from heat, stir in soured cream and seasoning, sprinkle with parsley.

Serve as side dish, or with wedge of brown bread for lunch.

COURGETTES

Go soft very quickly, need minimum cooking.

Wash and thinly slice, or cut into strips. Put in shallow boiling salt water for 2 - 3 minutes, drain immediately, add a knob of butter, black pepper and tarragon. (1 tsp tarragon approx 400g/1lb courgettes).
Serve with main course or as a starter.

Courgettes stuffed with Walnuts
à la Sarah

4 medium to large courgettes (or however many you need)
1 medium onion
50g/2oz chopped walnuts
50g/2oz breadcrumbs
25g/1oz butter
1 egg, beaten
1 tbsp tomato purée (paste)
1 tbsp chopped fresh sage (or 1tsp dried)
Salt & pepper
1 carton soured or fresh cream
Chopped parsley (optional)

Oven: Gas no. 5. 375°F. 190°C.
Ovenproof dish

Method

1. Wipe courgettes, cut down lengthwise one side, take out some of the centre to form a hollow (keep what you have removed).
2. Blanch in boiling salt water 3 - 4 minutes, drain, run under cold water, cool.
3. Put butter in pan, add chopped onion, cook until soft, remove from heat, add breadcrumbs, walnuts, egg, tomato purée, sage, seasoning and pulp removed from courgette and mix well.
4. Put good helping of this mixture into centre of each courgette, place in buttered ovenproof dish, dot with butter (if any mixture over, make into a ball, and put to cook).

Bake for 25 - 30 minutes.

When cooked pour cream and chopped parsley over courgettes.
Lovely as a vegetarian meal.

Courgette Casserole

6 medium courgettes, washed and cut into ¼" slices
100g/4oz butter
2 cloves garlic, crushed
200g/8oz mushrooms, sliced
50g/2oz brown breadcrumbs
400g/1lb tomatoes, skinned & chopped (or tin tomatoes, drained)
2 cartons soured cream
1 tbsp chopped almonds
1 tsp paprika
50g/2oz parmesan cheese

Oven: Gas no. 4. 350°F. 180°C.
Ovenproof dish

Method

1. Melt 75g/3oz butter in pan, when hot add enough sliced courgettes to cover base, cook 1 - 2 minutes, turning so each side is brown.
2. Remove and put into large mixing bowl. Continue until all courgettes are browned.
3. Add remaining butter to pan, melt, put in mushrooms and garlic, and stir frequently for 2 - 3 minutes. Now add tomatoes, soured cream, paprika, almonds and seasoning. Cook 1 - 2 minutes until well mixed.
4. Put all mixture with courgettes, fold together, spoon into casserole dish, sprinkle with parmesan. Cook in oven for 20 - 30 minutes. Serve with wholemeal noodles or spaghetti.

Ratatouille or "Ratatoo for Ray"

This is a simplified ratatouille, but is lovely and you can use up overgrown courgettes or marrow as well as young ones. Makes a lovely cheap lunch with chunks of brown bread.

600g/1½ courgettes (large or small)
400g/1lb tomatoes (or tin of tomatoes)
1 medium onion
2 cloves garlic
1 tbsp tomato paste or purée
1 tbsp chopped parsley
Cooking oil
Black pepper & salt

Method

1. Melt oil in large pan, slice onion, sauté until soft.
2. Take ends off courgettes, slice, or chop up into 2cm/1″ pieces, add to onion, with tomatoes, garlic, tomato paste, parsley and seasoning, mix well.
3. Simmer for about 20 minutes until veg are soft.

Serve as an accompaniment to main meal, or as lunch or supper with noodles, or bread. Or put some in ovenproof dish, sprinkle liberally with grated cheese, put in oven for 10 - 15 minutes. This Ratatoo can be done in large amounts when courgettes are in season. Keeps well in fridge for a week, or can be deep frozen to keep in freezer.

Courgettes à la Provençale

8 courgettes
4 tbsp olive oil
3 cloves garlic, crushed
50g/2oz dry breadcrumbs
2 tbsp chopped parsley
Black pepper & salt

Method

1. Cut courgettes into slices (crossways), pat dry.
2. Heat olive oil in pan, add courgettes, cook 6 - 8 minutes stirring to prevent sticking, raise heat, stir in salt, pepper, garlic, breadcrumbs & parsley, cook 2 - 3 minutes.
3. Remove pan from heat, transfer to warmed serving dish. Serve with meat, or as a light meal with brown bread.

Nutmeg Spinach

800g/2lb spinach, washed and chopped
50g/2oz butter
1 tsp ground nutmeg
Black pepper & salt

Method

1. Cook spinach in own water & salt, cook quickly until tender 6 - 8 minutes.
2. Drain and press well to extract all water, chop through.
3. Put into warmed serving dish, stir in nutmeg, pepper & salt — put butter on top.
Serve with brown rice.

Stir Fry Vegetables

This is a different method of cooking, traditionally Chinese, but has become very popular here. If you haven't a wok, a cast iron saucepan is best — though you can use an ordinary pan. The difference in the cooking is the heat of the oil, the speed of the cooking — you stir and fry all the time.

Preparation takes longest, as the vegetables must be prepared first.

Groundnut or sunflower oils are the best.

Any vegetables of your choice.

Carrots, peppers, mushrooms, cabbage, bean sprouts, etc. Soy sauce or sherry added towards the end of cooking adds flavour, also creates steam which finishes cooking the vegetables.

Method

1. Chop, slice or grate vegetables fairly thin.
2. Heat oil in wok or pan until hazy, (about 1 tbsp of oil).
3. Put vegetables in, putting those which will take longest first, then add others depending on how long they take — stir well all the time — 3 - 4 minutes is generally all that is needed.
4. Pour on either soy sauce or sherry (1 tbsp). Serve at once.

Examples:

5 - 6 minutes carrots,

3 minutes peppers, courgettes, shredded cabbage

2 minutes celery, bean shoots

Potato Crispy Skins

1kg/2lb potatoes | *Cummin seeds*
Salt | *Cooking oil*

Oven: Gas no. 5. 375°F. 190°C.

Method

1. Scrub potatoes, peel thickly, cut flesh into thin slices.
2. Put skins and flesh onto greased baking sheet, brush with oil. Sprinkle salt on to skins, cummin seeds on to flesh.
3. Bake in oven for 10 - 15 minutes, turning over to bake other side. Serve with dips.

Use hotter oven if you like browned, very crispy skins.

Dips

Mix 140ml/¼pt mayonnaise with 140ml/¼pt thick yogurt, clove garlic crushed & coriander.

Or, puree 1 avocado pear with juice ½ lemon and add 140ml/ ¼pt double cream or soured cream.

Vegetable Parcels Serves 4

1 pkt frozen puff pastry — size depending on quantity required, Small pkt makes 4

1 carrot & 1 parsnip
1 courgette, 2 sprigs broccoli
Few bean sprouts or celery (in fact any veg you have in)
25g/1oz grated cheese (leave out if not cheese eater)
Pepper & salt, few sesame seeds

Oven: Gas no. 6. 400°F. 200°C.
Baking Sheet

Method

1. Roll out pastry, cut into 4 squares about 15 x 15cm, (6 x 6").
2. Cook vegetables starting with carrots and parsnips, cook until tender, then add broccoli, sliced courgettes, bean sprouts, etc. Cook few minutes, drain well.
3. When cool put spoonfuls of vegetable on to each square of pastry, season, sprinkle on cheese, fold pastry over like a parcel, pick up gently, put on to greased baking sheet, folded side down, bake in oven for 10 - 15 minutes. Nice hot or cold.

Avocado & Bacon Salad

1 small crisp lettuce
2 avocado pears
3 - 4 rashers streaky bacon
Mustard vinaigrette — 1 tbsp wine vinegar
3 tbsp oil
1 tsp mustard

Method

1. Grill or fry bacon until very crisp, put aside to cool.
2. Mix together wine vinegar, oil, mustard, black pepper & salt, mix well, put aside.
3. Wash and shred lettuce.
4. Cut avocado in half, remove stone, peel & slice. Put shredded lettuce on plate, lay slices of avocado on lettuce, sprinkle vinaigrette over, top with crushed crispy bacon. Serve with brown bread.

AVOCADO is also delicious served sliced up with slices of orange on bed of lettuce.

Winter Salad

400g/1lb red cabbage
2 green apples
3 tbsp chopped parsley
100g/4oz red kidney beans
100g/4oz dried butter or haricot beans
juice of 2 lemons
70ml/2 ½oz vegetable or sunflower oil
Seasoning

Method

1. Beans can be prepared earlier if preferred.
Soak in cold water overnight, drain, boil until tender in water, about 1 hour, drain well, put aside.
2. Whisk together oil and lemon juice, season well, put beans into this dressing.
3. Apples cored, and thinly sliced, put in with beans.
4. Shred red cabbage fairly fine (don't use stem) and put this in with beans — cover and put to chill — stir in parsley before serving.

Ellide Salad

200g/½lb carrots, cooked }
400g/ 1lb potatoes, cooked } *do not overcook*
100g/4oz runner beans, cooked }
100g/4oz frozen peas
1 medium sized onion
1 medium sized eating apple
2 beetroot, cooked
2 cloves garlic
2 tbsp wine vinegar
50g/2oz mayonnaise (may need a little more)
4 tbsp chopped parsley
Black pepper & salt

Method

1. Cut into cubes the cooked cold potato, carrot, and beetroot, put into bowl, add runner beans and frozen peas, chopped onion and apple.
2. Add crushed garlic, mix with wine vinegar, mayonnaise and seasoning, put with vegetables and parsley, mix all together.

Most lovely salad and makes a wonderful hors d'ouevre. You can use any crisp vegetables such as celery or peppers but not too many soft vegetables.

Chicken & Nut Rice Salad

300g/12oz rice, cooked in usual way
6 tbsp olive oil
1 tsp wine vinegar
1 tsp mustard
100g/4oz cooked chicken
50g/2oz pecan nuts or walnuts, chopped
1 orange, peeled and sliced
1 tbsp fresh or dried tarragon
Salt & black pepper

Method

1. Put cooked rice in large bowl.
2. Mix together oil, vinegar and mustard, pour over rice, add chopped chicken pieces, nuts, orange and tarragon, season to taste, toss and serve.

Spinach & Mushroom Salad

400g/1lb spinach
200g/8oz mushrooms
1 finely chopped medium sized onion
1 tbsp chopped parsley
Black pepper & salt

Dressing

2 tbsp oil
1 tbsp wine vinegar
juice half lemon

Method

1. Wash, dry, despine the spinach, cut into 5mm/¼" size strips, put into bowl.
2. Slice mushrooms thinly, put with spinach, add chopped onion, parsley, pepper & salt, fold together.
3. Mix all dressing ingredients together, pour over salad just before serving.

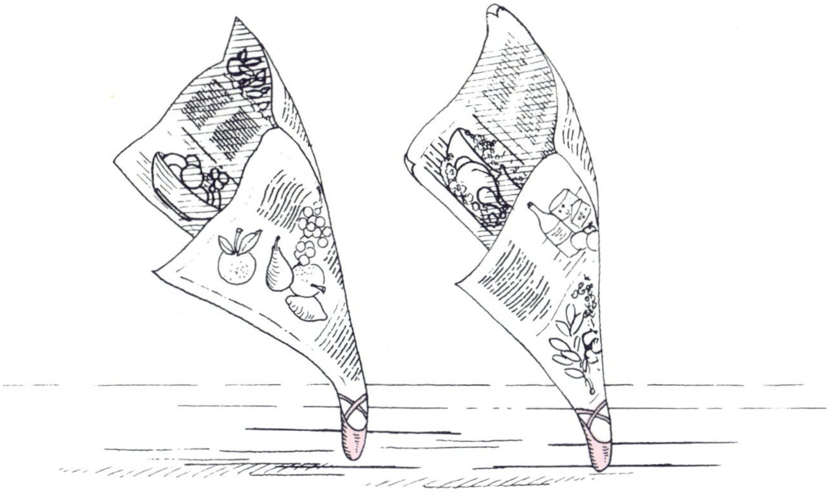

Fruit & Vegetables – 'Read all about them'

Courgette & Tuna Salad

200g/8oz tuna fish (tin)
2 tsp chopped parsley
2 hardboiled eggs, chopped
200g/8oz courgettes, sliced thinly and cooked
1 tbsp mayonnaise
1 tsp lemon juice
Black pepper & salt
1 iceberg lettuce or similar

Method

1. Parboil sliced courgettes, put in bowl, chop up hardboiled eggs, add to courgette.
2. Flake up tuna fish, mix with mayonnaise and lemon juice, add to the other mixture. Now put in parsley, pepper & salt.
3. Lay lettuce leaves round serving dish, put Tuna salad in centre of lettuce — chill.

PART 3

NUTS & PULSES

NUTS & PULSES

Recognised for their value for many, many years, in the Bible it mentions that, 'David was brought to eat Wheat, Barley, Corn, Beans & Lentils'.

These foods contain Protein, Iron, B Vitamins. They also have a low fat & high fibre content. Do make sure you clean, soak and COOK BEANS VERY WELL.

Do follow directions on packets when growing sprouting seeds.

PULSES & NUTS

Most pulses need washing first then SOAKING.

Long soak: which means leaving them in cold water overnight, or at least 6 - 8 hours.
Short hot soak: (if you have forgotten to soak overnight). Put into saucepan, bring to boil, boil for 6 - 8 minutes, remove from heat, leave to soak as they are for 1 hour.
Rinsing: After soaking, all beans (pulses) should be put in sieve or colander and rinsed thoroughly under cold water tap.

COOKING: do NOT add salt, it toughens skins. Boil in saucepan, covered generously with water.
Soaked Lentils, Peas: at least 20 - 30 minutes.
Red Kidney Beans: 1 hour, boil RAPIDLY for first 10 minutes.
Chick Peas: 2 hours.
Soya Beans: 3 - 4 hours.
Most Other Beans: 1 - 1½ hours.
Split lentils: do not need soaking.

Lentil & Courgette Flan

200g/8oz split green lentils
50g/2oz wholemeal flour
75g/3oz butter
200g/8oz courgettes
1 tbsp olive or sesame oil
Clove of garlic
2 eggs & 4 tbsp milk
150g/6oz soft cream cheese
50g/2oz grated hard cheese

Oven: Gas no. 5. 375°F. 190°C.
Flan case 21cm/8"

Method

1. Grind dry lentils in Magimix or grinder.
2. Put in bowl with flour, rub in butter, add enough water to just allow the mixture to come together. Press mixture into a flan case, and up sides, put to chill.
3. Blind bake for 20 minutes (put oven up to gas no.
6. 400°F. 200°C.)
4. Heat oil in pan, add sliced courgettes & garlic, cook 4 - 5 minutes, put into baked case.
5. Mix together cream cheese, beaten eggs and milk until blended, season to taste, pour over courgettes, sprinkle with grated cheese.
6. Bake until light brown, 20 - 25 minutes.

Soya Bean & Egg Croquettes

100g/4oz soya beans, soaked, rinsed & cooked until tender (best done day before)
1 onion, peeled and chopped
25g/1oz butter
3 hardboiled eggs
50g/2oz brown breadcrumbs
1 tbsp tomato paste
Dash worcester sauce
1 beaten egg
Oil for frying
Egg & breadcrumbs for coating

Method

1. Fry onion and garlic in butter for 10 minutes, remove from heat.
2. Mash cooked soya beans, add to pan, chop hardboiled eggs, add to mixture plus breadcrumbs, tomato paste, worcester sauce, beaten egg and seasoning, mix well.
3. Shape into croquettes, dip in egg and breadcrumbs.
4. Put oil in pan, when hot, fry croquettes until brown, drain on kitchen paper.

Serve with tomato sauce, or cold with mayonnaise and salad.

Haricot Beans in Cream

100g/4oz haricot beans } *or just one sort*
100g/4oz butter beans } *if preferred*
140ml/¼ pint double cream
2 tbsp chopped parsley
1 tbsp chopped chives or tarragon or mint
2 tsp lemon juice
1oz butter
drop white wine if available
Black pepper & salt

Method

1. Cook beans as normal (see beginning of this section). Drain well.
2. Fry onion in butter until soft, add cooked beans, keep on low heat, add cream, seasoning, herbs, lemon juice and wine, fold together.
3. Pour into serving dish, sprinkle with parsley or grated cheese.

Hummus

100g/4oz chick peas
2 cloves garlic
2 tbsp tahini (sesame cream)
Juice of 1 lemon
4 tbsp olive oil
Salt
Lemon wedges & paprika

Method

1. Soak, rinse and cook chick peas (1½ hours) until tender.

2. Strain, reserving some of the liquid.
3. Liquidize chick peas, add crushed garlic, lemon juice, tahini, half the olive oil and some of the cooking liquid, liquidize until smooth, add seasoning.
4. Put onto shallow dish — chill. Pour remaining olive oil over top, sprinkle with paprika.
Garnish with lemon wedges.
Serve with salad — or as a dip with raw vegetables & fruit.

Split Pea & Parsnip Pie

300g/12oz split green or yellow peas
600g/1 ½lb parsnips
2 onions
600g/1 ½lb potatoes
280ml/½pt milk
100g/4oz grated cheese
2 tsp mixed dried herbs
2 tbsp olive oil
25g/1oz butter
Seasoning

Oven: Gas no. 5. 375°F. 190°C.
Ovenproof pie dish

Method

1. Cook split peas until tender (approx ¾ hour).
2. Mash, sieve or liquidize them with the milk.
3. Heat oil in pan, add chopped onion, sauté until tender, add sliced parsnip, cover and cook until soft.
4. Meanwhile, boil potatoes, drain, then mash with butter, seasoning and mixed herbs.

5. Add split pea purée to parsnip and onion mixture, put into greased pie dish, top with the mashed potato, sprinkle on grated cheese.
6. Bake approx 30 minutes, until brown.
Serve with salad.

Vegetable & Nut Crumble

Topping

100g/4oz butter or margarine
175g/6oz wholemeal flour
100g/4oz grated cheese
50g/2oz chopped nuts (any sort)

Base

600g/1½lb mixed root vegetables (carrot, swede, parsnip, potato)
1 onion
50g/2oz butter or margarine
200g/8oz tomatoes, or tin tomatoes
280ml/ ½ pint vegetable stock
2 tbsp milk
25g/1oz flour
Pepper & salt

Oven: Gas no. 5. 375°F. 190°C.
Casserole dish

Method

Topping:

1. Rub fat into flour until fine crumbs, add cheese and nuts. Set aside.

Base:

2. Melt butter in pan, add chopped onion and sauté until tender.
3. Add skinned and sliced root vegetables, cook for 10 minutes.
4. Stir in flour, then add tomatoes, stock, milk and seasoning, bring to boil, simmer 10 minutes.
5. Transfer to ovenproof casserole dish, put crumble topping on.

Bake for 20 - 30 minutes until golden.

Vegetable Lasagne

8 strips wholewheat or green lasagne
1 onion, chopped
2 tbsp olive oil
1 clove garlic, crushed
200g/8oz mushrooms, sliced
400g/1lb tomatoes, or tin tomatoes
200g/8oz courgettes, sliced
3 tsp oregano
1 tsp nutmeg
3 tsp tomato purée

Sauce

25g/1oz butter
280ml/½ pint milk
25g/1oz flour
Parmesan cheese
Black pepper & salt

Oven: Gas no. 4. 350°F. 180°C.
Shallow ovenproof dish

Method

1. Cook lasagne in boiling salt water with few drops of olive oil for 10 minutes, or until tender, drain, and rinse with cold water, dry with cloth. (Pre-cooked lasagne is now available).
2. Fry onion in oil, add crushed garlic, mushrooms, courgettes, tomatoes (skinned if fresh & chopped) oregano, tomato purée, nutmeg, cover and cook for 10 - 15 minutes.
3. Meanwhile melt butter for sauce in pan add flour and milk making sure it does not go lumpy. Add seasoning, stir constantly for 5 minutes.
4. Grease a shallow ovenproof dish, put in half the vegetable mixture, half the lasagne, half the sauce, then repeat until dish is full. Sprinkle parmesan cheese on top.
5. Bake in oven 30 - 40 minutes until brown.

Margaret's Nut Loaf

2 leeks
50g/2oz mushrooms
2 cloves garlic
50g/2oz margarine
½tsp basil
½tsp celery seed
1 tsp Marmite
1 heaped tbsp plain flour
140ml/ ¼ pint water or stock
2 eggs, beaten
200g/8oz ground walnuts or hazelnuts
100g/4oz soft brown breadcrumbs
Salt & black pepper

Oven: Gas no. 4. 350°F. 180°C.
450g/1lb loaf tin

Method

1. Chop finely the leeks and mushrooms, crush the garlic.
2. Put margarine in frying pan, add leeks, mushrooms, garlic, celery seed and herbs, sauté until lightly browned.
3. Stir in Marmite and flour, add water, stir, then cook until thickened, add beaten eggs, cook a further 2 minutes, add breadcrumbs, nuts and seasoning.
4. Put into greased loaf tin, cover with foil, cook for 1 hour.

INTERMISSION AT THE BARRE

CAKES & PASTRIES

Note! Chocolate cakes in scenes 'Corps de Chocolate' and 'Chocolate Reverence'

Programme Notes

"There is no love sincerer than the love of food"

G. B. Shaw

INTERMISSION, 'an interval, a pause', so goes the definition. During this time as you indulge, both front and backstage with tasty sweet morsels, and imbibe champagne, I trust you will look back on the first half of this programme with pleasure, and eagerly anticipate that which is yet to be.

Enjoy your indulgence, then on to Act 2.

Contemporary Apple Cake

600g/1½lbs cooking apples
250g/10oz self raising flour
1 tsp baking powder
200g/8oz caster sugar
3 eggs
1 tsp almond essence
125g/5oz butter (melted)

Oven: Gas no. 4. 350°F. 180°C.
8" spring release loose bottom cake tin

Method

1. Line or butter an 8" loose bottom cake tin.
2. Put flour, baking powder and sugar into a bowl, beat eggs together, add to flour and sugar, then add the melted butter (mixture is rather thick), put in almond essence, mix well.
3. Meanwhile peel and thinly slice the apples.
4. Put half the cake mixture into bottom of cake tin, the sliced apples on top, then remaining half of cake mixture on top of apples, sprinkle with demerara sugar, and bake in oven approximately 1½ hours until golden brown.
5. Turn out of tin when cool, serve with fresh cream.

Jazzy Apple Cake

Base

150g/6oz self raising flour
50g/2oz soft brown sugar
50g/2oz ground almonds
75g/3oz butter
1 tsp lemon juice
½ beaten egg

Filling

400g/1lb cooking apples
3oz soft brown sugar
1 tsp lemon juice

Topping

50g/2oz self raising flour
125g/5oz soft brown sugar
1 tsp powdered cinnamon
50g/2oz butter

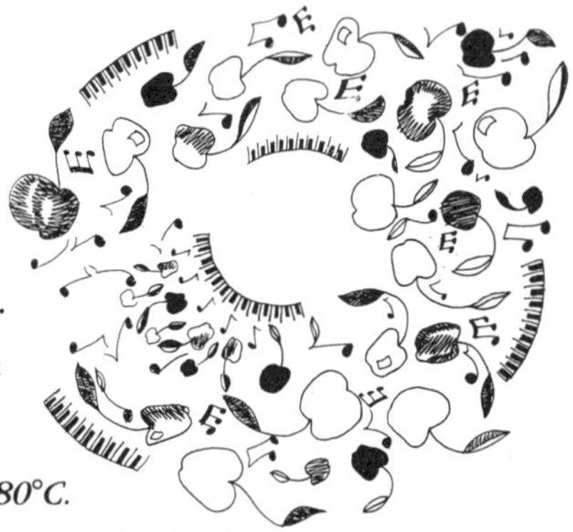

Oven: Gas no. 4. 350°F. 180°C.
8" loose bottom spring release cake tin

Method

Butter an 8" loose bottom cake tin

Base: Sift together the flour, sugar and ground almonds, rub in the butter until the mixture is like fine breadcrumbs, mix to a stiff consistency with lemon juice and egg — press into base of cake tin and set aside to chill.

Filling: Peel, core and slice apples, put into a bowl with the sugar and lemon juice, mix well, then put on cake base.

Topping: Rub butter into the mixed flour, sugar and cinnamon until it resembles fine breadcrumbs, sprinkle over top of apples, press down. Bake approximately 1¼ hours until light brown on top.

Note: A sprinkle of muesli over the top of the cake, put on half way through the cooking time gives a nice crunchy top.

Cheesecake (I use Philadelphia Cream Cheese)

Pastry Base

200g/8oz plain flour
75g/3oz butter
50g/2oz lard
25g/1oz icing sugar
1 egg
2 tbsp cold water

Filling

125g/5oz butter
150g/6oz caster sugar
4 eggs
25g/10oz plain flour
Zest and juice of 2 lemons
1 tsp vanilla essence
600g/1½lbs soft cream cheese
4 tbsp milk

Topping

Any fresh fruit in season or sliced dried fruit.
Oven: Gas no. 3. 325°F. 170°C.
9" loose bottom spring release cake tin

Method

Pastry base: Rub the butter & lard into the blended flour and icing sugar, beat the egg and cold water together, add a little at a time until pastry is a pliable dough. Roll out pastry on floured board, line the cake tin by cutting a circle of pastry to fit the bottom, then a strip to go all around the edge — put to chill.

Filling:

1. Cream butter and sugar until light and fluffy. Gradually add the beaten eggs — sprinkle in a little flour between each egg to prevent curdling. Add the lemon juice, zest and vanilla essence.
2. In another bowl beat the cream cheese until smooth, now add to the butter mixture, whisk until a pouring consistency — pour into the chilled pastry case.
3. Bake in oven 1½ hours approximately until set and light golden on top, sounds hollow when tapped. When cooked remove from oven cool slightly, release the springform tin then leave to cool completely.

Top with sliced fresh fruit.
Serve with cream.

Carol's Mother's Day Cheesecake

Torte crust for base

100g/4oz butter or margarine

150g/6oz plain flour

50g/2oz granulated sugar

½ tsp vanilla essence

Filling

400g/1lb cream cheese

50g/2oz granulated sugar

2 eggs (beaten)

½ tsp vanilla essence

Topping

3 medium eating apples (peeled and cored)

25g/1oz brown sugar

½ tsp cinnamon

50g/2oz coarse chopped walnuts

Oven: Gas no. 4. 350°F. 180°C.
9" spring release cake tin — buttered

Method

1. Cut butter into small pieces, combine butter with flour, sugar and vanilla, mix until it resembles fine breadcrumbs.
2. Press into base and halfway up sides of cake tin, bake for 5 minutes.

Filling:

3. In a large bowl combine cream cheese, sugar, eggs and vanilla essence, beat until smooth, pour into cooled pastry case.

Topping:

4. Mix together the sliced apples, sugar, cinnamon and chopped nuts — layer them on the top of cheesecake.
5. Bake for ½ hour, then reduce heat slightly if cooking too quickly, cook for further ½ hour.

Cool, then chill in fridge.

American Quick Cheesecake

Base

1½ cups crushed biscuit crumbs

6 tbsp melted butter

25g/1oz white sugar

Filling

400g/1lb cream cheese

50g/2oz granulated sugar

2 large eggs (beaten)

1 tsp vanilla essence

Topping

1 carton soured cream

2 tbsp granulated sugar

1 tsp vanilla essence

Oven: Gas no. 4. 350°F. 180°C.
9" pie dish or cake tin

Method

Base:

1. Place biscuit crumbs (crushed with rolling pin or in liquidizer) in a bowl with sugar, add melted butter, mix well.
2. Press into greased dish or tin over base and up sides, bake for 10 minutes, cool before filling.

Filling:

3. Beat together cheese, sugar, eggs and vanilla essence, pour into prepared and cooled crust, bake 20 minutes.

Topping:

4. Mix together soured cream, sugar and vanilla. Pour on top of cheesecake when cooked, return to oven for 5 - 7 minutes, cool, then chill.

Best kept overnight before cutting.

Very quick cheesecake to make, and delicious.

Lemon Cheesecake slices (makes 12)

100g/4oz shortcrust pastry
200g/8oz marzipan
75g/3oz cream cheese
2 eggs (separated)
Rind & juice of 1 lemon
50g/2oz caster sugar
1 tbsp plain flour
1 tbsp milk

Oven: Gas no. 3. 325°F. 170°C.
8″ shallow baking tray (square)

Method

1. Make the pastry and line the baking tray with it.
2. Divide the marzipan in half and roll two 8″ squares. Cover the pastry with one.
3. Cream the cheese, beat in the egg yolks, lemon rind & juice, sugar, flour and milk.
4. Whisk the egg whites and fold in to the mixture. Spread ½ of this onto the marzipan and pastry in tin, then cover with the other marzipan square, then remaining mixture.
5. Bake for 1 hour. When cool cut into slices and dust with icing sugar.

Yummy Honey Squares (Makes 9)

100g/4oz margarine
2 tbsp honey
175g/7oz plain flour

Filling

25g/1oz margarine
75g/3oz raisins
1 banana
2 tbsp milk
½ tsp cinnamon
1 tbsp caster sugar

Oven: Gas no. 5. 375°F. 190°C.
7" square shallow baking tin — one can, of course, use a round tin and call them Yummy Honey Slices!

Method

1. Melt the margarine and honey in a small pan, cool slightly, then add the flour. Knead this to a dough and chill for 15 minutes (should be a pliable dough). Add more flour if in doubt.
2. Melt the 'filling' margarine, add the milk and raisins and cook gently for 1 - 2 minutes, remove from heat.
3. Peel and slice the banana and add this with the cinnamon to the mixture. Cool.
4. Press half of the dough into a greased 7" square shallow baking tin, spread with the filling. Roll then slice the remaining dough, cut into about 15 slices — and lay them over the top. Sprinkle with caster sugar.

Bake for 35 - 40 minutes.
When cool cut into squares. Very nice indeed.

Passion Cake

250g/10oz plain flour
2 tsp baking powder
1 tsp bicarbonate of soda
1 tsp salt
3 eggs
50g/2oz chopped walnuts
2 bananas
150g/6oz soft brown sugar
170ml/6 fl.oz corn oil
150g/6oz carrots — finely grated

Filling & Frosting

150g/6oz icing sugar
75g/3oz cream cheese
150g/6oz butter
½ tsp vanilla essence

Oven: Gas no. 4. 350°F. 180°C.
9" greased cake tin

Method

1. Sift together the flour, baking powder, bicarbonate and salt. Add the walnuts and sugar.
2. Peel and mash the bananas and mix with the beaten eggs and grated carrot.
3. Now add the oil and dry ingredients and mix well. Pour into a greased cake tin and cook for approximately 40 minutes.

Remove from oven, when cool put on a wire rack.

Filling & Topping: mix all the ingredients together until soft and creamy and when the cake has cooled, cut in half through the middle. Spread half the mixture on, put halves back together, spread the remainder on top of the cake. Decorate if liked with walnuts.

Banana & Apricot Cake

1 tin apricot halves (drained)
2oz chopped walnuts
3 ripe bananas
2 carrots (peeled and grated)
150g/6oz light muscavado sugar
3 eggs
250g/10oz plain flour
1 tsp bicarbonate of soda
2 tsp baking powder
170ml/6 fl.oz corn oil

Icing

75g/3oz soft butter
75g/3oz cream cheese
175g/7oz icing sugar
½ tsp vanilla essence

Oven: Gas no. 5. 375°F. 190°C.
2lb loaf tin

Method

1. Mash apricots — leaving a few for decorations — blend with 2 mashed bananas, walnuts, carrots, sugar and eggs.
2. Sieve together the flour, salt, bicarbonate and baking powder and fold in to the apricot mixture. Pour in oil and mix well.
3. Pour into a greased and lined 2lb loaf tin and bake for approx 1 hour.

Topping:
4. Blend all the icing ingredients together, and when the cake is cold cut in half across the middle, put half the icing mixture in, sandwich together, then top with remaining icing.
Decorate with sliced banana and apricot.

Fruit & Oat Bars

100g/4oz hard margarine
2 tbsp golden syrup
2 tbsp black treacle
50g/2oz light brown sugar
50g/2oz hazelnuts (or nuts of your choice)
50g/2oz seedless raisins
150g/6oz porridge oats
50g/2oz wheatgerm
75g/3oz chopped dried apricots and dates
Honey to glaze

Oven: Gas no. 4. 350°F. 180°C.
Greased shallow baking tray

Method

1. Melt margarine, syrup, treacle and sugar together in pan, stir all remaining ingredients in to this.
2. Press into greased tin, bake 20 - 25 minutes. Cut into bars while still warm, and brush with honey. Leave in tin to cool.

Macaroons

125g/5oz caster sugar
125g/5oz ground almonds
2 egg whites
Few drops almond essence
Rice paper (edible)

Oven: Gas no. 4. 350°F. 180°C.
Baking Tray

Method

1. Whisk egg whites lightly until thick, but not stiff. Add almond essence, sugar and ground almonds.
2. Turn onto board, roll into a roll — cut into about 12 slices, place on rice paper on baking tray.
3. Bake 20 - 25 minutes until pale brown colour. When cool trim off extra rice paper, leaving just that on base of macaroons.

Florentines

100g/4oz butter
100g/4oz caster sugar
100g/4oz almonds (coarse chopped)
50g/2oz mixed peel
50g/2oz walnuts (chopped)
50g/2oz glacé cherries (chopped)
50g/2oz raisins
1 egg
75g/3oz plain chocolate

Oven: Gas no. 4. 350°F. 180°C.
Baking Tray

Method

1. Put butter and sugar into a pan, stir over gentle heat until melted, stir in all the other ingredients except the chocolate.
2. Put in small heaps on to the greased baking tray — (allow room to spread).
3. Bake for 20 minutes, cool, then remove very carefully onto a wire rack.
4. When completely cold coat the bottom of each florentine with melted chocolate, leave upside down until cold and chocolate set.

Apricot Shorties

150g/6oz butter
150g/6oz self raising flour
150g/6oz fine semolina
75g/3oz caster sugar
100g/4oz dried apricots (chopped & soaked for ½ hour)
Juice of ½ lemon
3 tbsp sugar
140ml/ ¼ pint water

Oven: Gas no. 5. 375°F. 190°C.
11" x 7" baking tray

Method

1. Chop up apricots, soak for ½ hour in hot water, drain. Put apricots, juice of lemon, 3 tbsp sugar and ¼ pint water into saucepan, simmer until soft (20 minutes).
2. Melt the margarine in pan, add sugar, flour and semolina, mix until like breadcrumbs.
3. Put half of this mixture in bottom of greased baking tray — press down, now spread apricot mixture on, then the remaining crumble on top, press lightly.
4. Bake in oven for 15 - 20 minutes, cut into squares, but leave in tin until cold.

Meringue Dreams (makes 16)

3 egg whites
100g/4oz soft light brown sugar
25g/1oz flaked almonds
140ml/ ¼ pint double cream

Oven: Gas no. ¼. 225°F. 110°C.
Baking tray

Method

1. Whisk egg whites until stiff, whisk in half the sugar, then fold in remaining sugar using a metal spoon.
2. Pipe 16 rings (about 3″ diameter) on to baking tray (preferably lined with non stick parchment). Sprinkle almonds over 8 of the rings.
3. Put in bottom of oven and bake until dry, about 1½ hrs.
4. When cool, carefully remove from baking dish. Sandwich together with whipped double cream, dust with icing sugar.

Light Lemon Cake

100g/4oz soft margarine
150g/6oz self raising flour
150g/6oz caster sugar
2 large eggs
4 tbsp milk
Grated rind of 1 lemon

Syrup

3 tbsp icing sugar warmed to a syrup with 3 tbsp lemon juice (1 large lemon)

Oven: Gas no. 4 350°F. 180°C.
Well greased 2lb loaf tin

Method

1. Beat margarine and sugar together until fluffy (or use mixer). Add eggs gradually, beat until light.
2. Fold in flour, lemon rind and milk.
3. Put in loaf tin and bake for 40 - 45 minutes. Remove from oven, leave in tin while you heat the icing sugar and lemon juice together.
4. Prick cake all over top with fork — gently pour syrup over. Leave until cold — turn out — dust with icing sugar.

Fruit Cake

100g/4oz self raising flour
100g/4oz plain wholemeal flour
½ tsp baking powder
100g/4oz margarine
100g/4oz brown sugar
2 eggs
300g/12oz mixed fruit (currants, sultanas, raisins, mixed peel)
1 tbsp thin honey or golden syrup
Pinch nutmeg or cinnamon
Small drop of milk

Oven: Gas no. 3. 325°F. 170°C.
8" greased and lined cake tin or 1lb loaf tin.

Method

1. Cream margarine and sugar.
2. Beat eggs with the milk, add gradually to the creamed mixture, also the honey or syrup.
3. Sift flour, baking powder and spices together. Fold into cake mixture.
4. Add fruit, mix well, put into cake tin.
5. Bake in centre of oven for 1¾ to 2 hours until skewer comes out clean. Leave in tin to cool.

The Carrot Cake

Cake

250g/9oz wholemeal, or white self raising flour
350g/12oz soft brown sugar
3 large eggs
175ml/6 fl.oz sunflower oil
1 teaspoon bicarbonate of soda
2 teaspoons vanilla essence
1 teaspoon ground nutmeg
2 teaspoons cinnamon
pinch salt
300g/11oz grated carrot
75g/3oz desiccated coconut

Topping

75g/3oz sifted icing sugar
juice of half lemon

Oven Gas No. 2. 300°F. 150°C.
8" greased and lined cake tin.

Method

1. Place eggs, oil and vanilla essence in a bowl, add sugar and mix well.
2. In another bowl mix together sieved flour, nutmeg, cinnamon, salt and bicarbonate of soda.
3. Next fold the flour mixture into the wet ingredients in first bowl, then add grated carrot and coconut and mix well.
4. Place in prepared cake tin, bake on centre shelf of oven 1½ - 2 hours.

When cake is cold, squeeze lemon juice into sieved icing sugar, until spreading consistency — then spread over top of cake.
Very thin strips of orange peel are nice to decorate this cake.

Plum & Almond Tart

100g/4oz shortcrust pastry
100g/4oz butter or margarine
100g/4oz caster sugar
1 egg, separated, plus 1 extra egg yolk
100g/4oz self raising flour
2 tbsp milk
2 tbsp lemon juice
25g/1oz ground almonds
1 tsp almond essence
6 tbsp plum jam
Flaked almonds to decorate

Oven: Gas no. 4. 350°F. 180°C.
8" cake tin, greased

Method

1. Roll out pastry, line greased tin with the pastry, prick well. Bake blind in hot oven Gas 6. 400°F. 200°C. for 10 minutes.
2. Whisk together butter and sugar until light and fluffy, gradually add egg yolks then stir in ground almonds and almond essence.
3. Fold in flour, lemon juice and milk.
4. Whisk egg whites until stiff, fold into mixture.
5. Spread plum jam over pastry base, spoon over the cake mixture, sprinkle almond flakes on top, bake in oven until golden brown, approximately 30 minutes.

Fruit Tart

Danish Pastries

1 level tsp caster sugar (for yeast)
5 tbsp warm water
1 ½ level tsp dried yeast
25g/1oz lard
200g/8oz plain flour
1 beaten egg
125g/5oz butter
12g/ ½oz caster sugar
Pinch salt

Fillings

Almond paste
Currants/peel
Sugar/cinnamon

Oven: Gas no. 6. 400°F. 200°C.
Baking Tray

Method

1. Add the tsp caster sugar to the warm water, when dissolved sprinkle yeast on top and leave in a warm place until frothy, about 10 minutes.
2. Rub lard into flour and salt, make a well in centre of flour and stir in the yeast mixture, beaten egg and sugar, mix to a soft dough (I use a knife to mix this).
3. Put on to a floured board and knead well, until smooth. Place dough in a polythene bag and leave to rest for 10 - 15 minutes.
4. Meanwhile, work the butter until it is a long oblong block, about 9″ x 3″. Roll out the dough to a 10″ square, put butter in centre, fold over each side, seal top and bottom edges, roll out to about 16″ square, fold over edge again, then roll out, repeat this twice more. Leave dough to rest in cool place for ½ hour.

Almond Triangles

Roll out pastry to a 16″ square (roughly), cut in half, cut one half into 4″ squares, put a piece of almond paste in centre of each, fold over diagonally to form a triangle. Seal edges with water, place on baking tray, bake 15 - 20 minutes. Cool on wire rack.

Fruit Wheels

Roll out other half of pastry, cut into 2 pieces, spread each piece with a mixture of 25g/1oz butter, 25g/1oz sugar, 1 tsp cinnamon mixed together. Scatter a few currants and mixed peel on top. Roll up, then slice into 1″ slices, so they look like wheels.

Place on a baking tray and bake for 10 - 15 minutes. Cool on wire rack.

Mince Pies (Makes approximately 15)

Mince Pie Pastry

100g/4oz plain flour

100g/4oz self raising flour

50g/2oz Trex or lard

50g/2oz hard margarine (Echo)

1 tbsp caster sugar

Pinch salt

Water to mix

Jar mincemeat

Oven: Gas no. 6. 400°F. 200°C.

Pastry tins (patty tins)

Method

1. Put flour into bowl with salt and sugar. Rub in the Trex and margarine, until mixture resembles fine breadcrumbs.

Add water a little at a time until you have a good working dough.
2. Turn out on to a floured board, roll out pastry. Using round pastry cutters, cut 15 large (to fit bottom of tins), and 15 small (for tops).
3. Put pastry bases into patty tins, put tsp of mincemeat into each one. Slightly wet one side of small rounds and put on top of mincemeat, press.
4. Dust with caster sugar, put in oven for approximately 10 - 15 minutes. Cool on wire rack.

One can get very miniature patty tins, which make lovely 'one bite' size mince pies.

Scones (Makes 12 – 14)

200g/8oz self raising flour
1/4 tsp salt
50g/2oz butter
12g/1/2oz sugar
1 egg
milk to mix

Oven: Gas no. 5. 375°F. 190°C.
Baking Tray

Method

1. Sieve flour and salt, rub in butter, add sugar, then mix with beaten egg and milk until you have a soft dough.
2. Turn on to a floured board and roll out to about 1″ thick, cut round shapes with 2 cutter, put onto greased baking sheet.
3. Brush tops with milk — bake 10 - 15 minutes until well risen and golden.

Serve with butter and homemade jam, and cream.

To make farmhouse scones add 50g/2oz sultanas to the above mixture.

Wholemeal flour can be used if preferred to make wholemeal scones, mixture as above.

Quick Soda Bread

200g/8oz wholemeal flour
200g/8oz white flour
1 tsp bicarbonate of soda
1 tsp cream of tartar
25g/1oz margarine
280ml/½ pint sour milk or sweet milk (add a drop of vinegar to milk to make it sour)
½ beaten egg

Oven: Gas no. 4. 350°F. 180°C.
Baking Tray

Method

1. Sieve together flour, bicarbonate of soda and cream of tartar, rub in the margarine, make a well in centre of flour, pour in milk, making a soft spongy dough.
2. Turn on to a floured board, shape into 2 rounds, brush top with beaten egg.
3. Bake 30 - 40 minutes until hollow sound when tapped on bottom.

Somerset Tea Loaf

250g/10oz mixed dried fruit (prepared previous night — see below)
2 eggs
140ml/¼ pint cold tea
100g/4oz brown sugar
150g/6oz self raising flour
½ tsp mixed spice

Oven: Gas no. 3. 325°F. 170°C.
1lb loaf tin, lined and greased

Method

1. Pour cold tea over mixed fruit and leave overnight.
2. Beat eggs, add to fruit with sugar, flour & spice, it may seem runny but this is alright — pour into tin.
3. Bake — middle — shelf for approximately 1 hour. Cool on a wire rack.

Serve cold cut into slices and buttered.

Banana Teabread

200g/8oz self raising flour
¼ tsp bicarbonate of soda
½ tsp salt
75g/3oz butter
150g/6oz caster sugar
2 beaten eggs
400g/1lb bananas (mashed)
100g/4oz nuts (chopped)

Oven: Gas no. 4. 350°F. 180°C.
1lb loaf tin, lined and greased

Method

1. Sift together flour, soda and salt, cream butter and sugar, add eggs, beat well, add mashed banana and beat, stir in flour and nuts.
2. Put mixture into tin, bake for 1¼ hours.
3. Turn on to wire rack to cool.

Serve cold cut into slices.

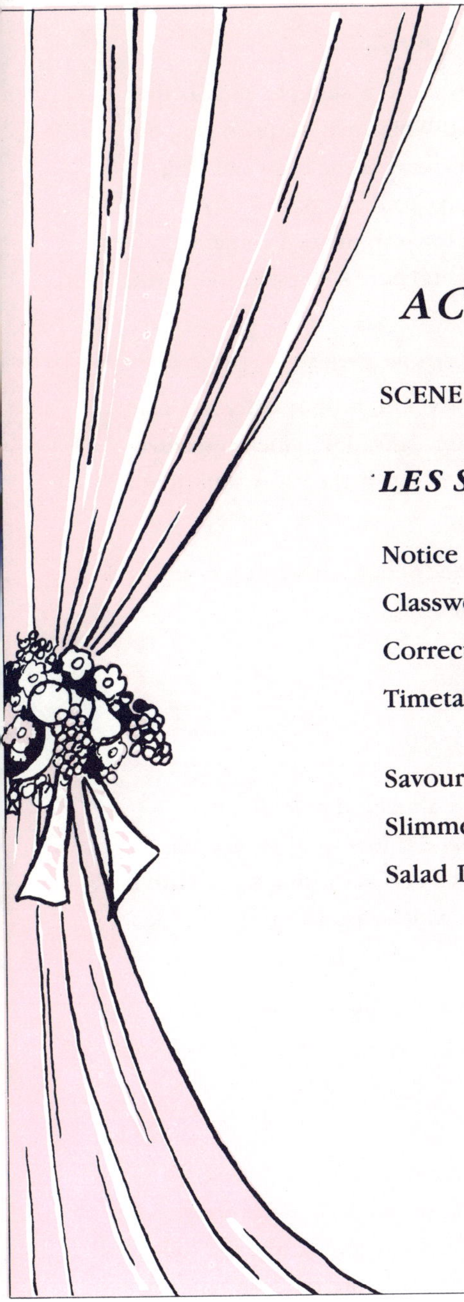

ACT 2

SCENE 1

LES SYLPHIDES

NOTICE BOARD

'Les Sylphides', the scene for those wishing to slim, is the slimmest section of this book! Which may surprise you, but I firmly believe that sensible eating is the basis of being slim, so, if you turn a blind eye to the contents of the scenes you know are wrong for you, the rest contain recipes for a well balanced diet. I have suggested some, you can choose the rest.

Those of you who are overweight, yet always hungry, do not fear, food can be filling and fun, yet not fattening. Like your dancing there are no short cuts, discipline is essential, but has its rewards, for you will satisfy the inner soul, if not the inner man!

DO NOT let an overweight body come between you and your chosen way of life — dancing.

Lose weight — then maintain it.

WORKSHOP NOTES

I must establish that I am not a medical person, or a nutritionalist, and I do not intend to give diets as such, neither do I believe them to be necessary unless you have a specific weight 'problem', in which case you should seek a doctor's advice.

The habit of overeating, picking, using convenience foods, builds up slowly, without you realising it, so you now have to re-train both your body and mind to a new way of eating.

Dancing takes a tremendous amount of energy, be it contemporary, classical, modern, jazz or tap, a professional dancer works long, physically exhausting hours, the right foods are essential for you all, to restore the loss and damage your bodies suffer, and it is even more important for those of you who want to keep their weight down, to eat correctly.

Sudden withdrawal of essential foods, in an effort to lose weight quickly can cause fatigue, headaches and lack of coordination.

As a guide —

Daily intake should be

⅓ Body building foods
Meat, fish, eggs, cheese, nuts, poultry

⅓ Protective foods
Fruit, vegetables, dairy produce

⅓ Energy foods
Bread, cakes, puddings, preserves & chocolate

CORRECTIONS

NO to

Sweets, cakes, puddings, cream, packet foods, peanuts, crisps, beefburgers, sausages, chips, white bread, white sugar, biscuits, squashes, fizzy drinks, alcohol, blended oils, butter, tinned fruit and vegetables and chocolate!

YES to

Lean meat, chicken, steak, liver, fish — preferably white fish, low fat cheeses, eggs, skimmed milk, pulses, nuts, vegetables, fruit, wholemeal bread, wholemeal flour and pasta, brown rice, high fibre cereals, low fat cream, low fat yogurts, vegetable oils, margarine, carob, mineral waters, unsweetened fresh fruit drinks.

LEARN to

Grill foods, not fry.
Trim fat off meat and bacon before cooking, then skim off any residue while cooking.

Use lemon juice & herbs in place of salt.

Replace cream with low fat yoghurt or quark.

Use half milk and water for sauces.

Make pastry with wholemeal flour and sunflower margarine.

Read labels on tins and packets for hidden fats and sugar.

Eat quality not quantity.

Chocolate, if you cannot live without it, ration yourself to child size bars, only 1 or 2 a week.

TIMETABLE — Suggestions as such, not a diet.

Drink

Black, unsweetened coffee or tea
Unsweetened fruit juices
Spa and tap water
1 or 2 glasses wine only at weekends.

Breakfast suggestions

Don't miss this meal, it is very important.

1. *Boiled egg, 1 slice wholemeal toast — drink.*
2. *Apple muesli, 1 slice wholemeal toast — drink.*
3. *Poached haddock (4oz) 1 slice brown bread — drink.*
4. *1 rasher grilled bacon & 2 tomatoes, ryvita — drink.*
5. *Fruit compôte & grapefruit, wheat flakes — drink.*

Lunch suggestions

To take to class or theatre

1. *Tuna & Egg Salad, banana and drink.*
2. *Cheese & ryvita, dried apricots — drink.*
3. *Slice nut loaf, lettuce, cucumber, apple — drink.*
4. *Hardboiled egg, tomato, yogurt — drink.*

To eat at home

1. *Soup, wholemeal bread, apple or orange — drink.*
2. *Omelette (1 egg), watercress, fruit & nuts — drink.*
3. *Stir fry vegetables, cheese — drink.*
4. *100g/4oz grilled fish, ryvita, coffee jelly — drink.*

Keep cut up raw vegetables ready to nibble at when desperate.

Dinner suggestions

1. 100g/4oz grilled lean steak, 1 potato, green salad.
Apricot fool, small slice cheese — drink.
2. 100g/4oz white fish grilled or poached, courgettes and carrots.
Carob pudding — drink.
3. 2 slices nut loaf or nut crumble, grilled mushrooms and tomatoes.
Junket or plain yogurt — drink.
4. Breast of chicken (100g/4oz), 1 potato, broccoli and parsnip
Fresh fruit salad — drink.
5. Omelette (2 eggs), mixed salad. Caramelized orange.
Small slice cheese — drink.

Selected Savoury Recipes from other Scenes

ACT 1

Scene 2 **Warm ups**
Soups
Pâté

Scene 3 **Principal Dishes**
Steaks
Grilled chicken & almonds
Liver & bacon

Scene 4 **Dancing with Soul**
Stir fried prawns with broccoli
Grilled trout with almonds
White fish — grilled or poached

Scene 5 **Variations**
Tuna & Egg Salad
Spinach & Mushroom Salad
Ratatouille
Express Cheese Supper
Courgettes
Hummus
Soya Bean & Egg Croquettes
Nut Loaf
Vegetable & Nut Crumble

DESSERTS FOR SLIMMERS

Junket

570ml/1 pint milk — low fat
1 tbsp caster sugar
1 tsp rennet essence
Grated nutmeg

Method

1. Heat the milk until just warm, remove from heat, stir in sugar until dissolved, then add rennet essence.
2. Pour into serving dish, leave for 1 - 2 hours, undisturbed until set.
3. Grate nutmeg on top, chill in fridge.

Carob Pudding

230ml/8 fl.oz warm water
1 tsp gelatine
3 tbsp honey
2 tbsp carob powder
90ml/3 fl.oz vegetable oil
1 tsp vanilla essence
2 eggs

Method

1. Blend warm water and gelatine, whisk until it dissolves.
2. Put the honey, carob, oil, vanilla and eggs into the gelatine. Whisk, or put in a blender and blend well together.
3. Pour into a dish, or mould, put to chill in the fridge.

Honey Baked Apple

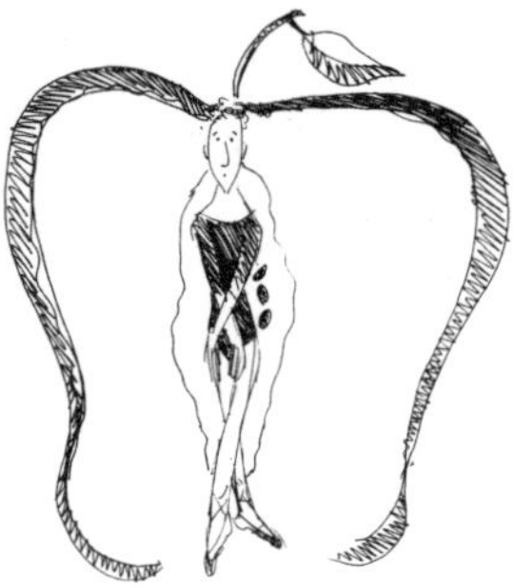

1 large cooking apple
25g/1oz brown breadcrumbs
1 tsp honey
1 tsp lemon juice
25g/1oz raisins & walnuts mixed

Oven: Gas no. 6. 400°F. 200°C. 30 minutes.

Method

1. Core the apple, and slit skin slightly all round the top of the apple (to allow for splitting).
2. Mix the breadcrumbs and fruit & nuts together. Add the honey and lemon juice and press into the centre of the apple — press down firmly.
3. Place on greased baking tray or foil dish, bake until tender.

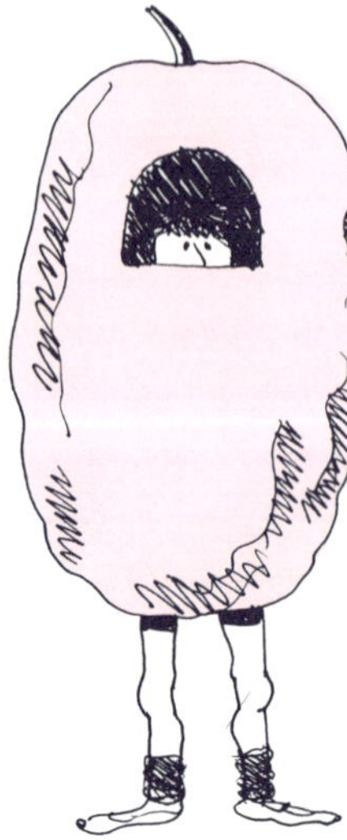
Apricot Fool

Apricot Fool

400g/1lb dried apricots
300g/12oz quark
2 tbsp honey

Method

1. Soak the apricots.
2. Drain and put in blender with the quark and honey. Blend until smooth and chill before serving.

Coffee Jelly

1 pkt gelatine
1 pint sweetened coffee
1 tsp sherry or brandy
Cream to serve if allowed

Method

1. Make up coffee to strength desired, using fresh or instant coffee, add brown sugar & sherry and sprinkle on the gelatine, stir until dissolved.
2. When cooled a little, pour into individual glasses, then stand them on a surface and put something under each glass so that jelly sets at an angle.
3. To serve, fill the space left at the side of jelly with whipped cream or chopped dried fruit if cream not allowed.

Dried Fruit Compôte

300g/12oz dried fruit, apricots, pears, apple, prunes
2 tbsp brown sugar
1 3⁄4 pints tea, freshly made
Grated rind of 1 orange
Juice of 1 lemon
Pinch nutmeg *Oven: Gas no. 1. 275°F. 140°C.*

Method

1. Wash fruit and put in an ovenproof dish with the hot tea, cover with lid or foil, put in oven for approximately 1 hour until fruit is soft.
2. Strain off juice into a saucepan, put fruit into a serving dish, sprinkle with pinch nutmeg.
3. Add orange rind, lemon juice and sugar to fruit juices, bring to boil, simmer 5 - 10 minutes.
4. Pour this juice over the fruit.
5. Put to chill — decorate with flaked almonds.

Raspberry Snow

400g/1lb fresh or frozen raspberries (or 1 can)
2 egg whites

Method

1. Wash and cook raspberries in a very little water. When cool, drain liquid into a jug, put raspberries through a sieve. (Frozen or canned do not need cooking).
2. Put purée into an ice tray, place in freezer for 30 minutes.
3. Beat the egg whites until peaks form.
4. Take raspberries out of freezer, put in bowl, add egg white, fold together.
5. Serve in individual dishes, topped with 1 spoonful of natural yogurt and a few toasted almonds.

Apple Meusli

280ml/½ pint milk - low fat
1 eating apple
Juice of 1 lemon
1 tsp honey
50g/2oz rolled oats

Method

1. Put milk and apple, cored and cut into pieces, into a liquidizer, turn on and liquidize until apple is in very small pieces.
2. Now add lemon juice and honey, liquidize for 1 minute.
3. Put oats into a dish, pour on the apple mixture, stir -leave for ½ hour.

This keeps for 2 - 3 days in fridge, so you can make enough to last that time. Good for breakfast, or as a dessert.

Quick Caramelized Oranges

1 orange
25g/1oz demerara sugar
1 tsp sherry (optional)

Method

1. Put sugar into a small foil dish, place under hot grill until melted, (keep an eye on it, or it will burn). Remove when bubbling, put aside to cool.
2. Peel orange, remove all pith, slice very thinly, and arrange in a dish (put sherry on now if using).
3. Sugar (caramelized) is now cold, and will easily be removed from foil. Break in pieces and scatter on top of orange slices.

Serve with soured cream.

Fatless Fruit Cake

200g/8oz dried fruit
50g/2oz honey
6 tbsp fruit juice
150g/6oz wholemeal plain flour
2 tsp baking powder
½ tsp spices
pinch nutmeg
1 egg
Oven: Gas no. 3. 325°F. 170°C.

Method

1. Mix the fruit with the honey and fruit juice. Add the beaten egg. Sieve the flour, baking powder and spices and mix well with the fruit mixture.
2. Pour into a 1lb loaf tin and bake for approximately 1 hr.
3. Cook on wire rack — dust with icing sugar.

SALAD DRESSING FOR SLIMMERS

Honey & Lemon Dressing

(Nice with fruit based salads)

Juice of 1 lemon
2 tbsp clear honey
Salt & pepper

Method

Whisk all ingredients together.

Yogurt Dressing

140ml/5fl.oz. (¼ pint) natural yogurt
½ tsp brown sugar or honey
Grated rind and juice of ½ a lemon
1 tbsp finely chopped onion
Salt & pepper

Method

Combine all ingredients, season to taste.

Low Calorie Dressing

2 tbsp lemon juice
2 tbsp fresh orange juice
2 tsp chopped parsley or chives
1 tsp mixed mustard
Black pepper & salt

Method

Whisk all ingredients together until well blended, serve with salad or vegetables.

Yogurt Mayonnaise

2 tbsp plain low fat yogurt
1 tbsp oil
1 tbsp white wine vinegar
1 tsp mayonnaise
Black pepper

Method

Blend all ingredients together in a bowl using a whisk or a fork, put in fridge until required.

ACT 2

SCENE 2

DRESSING UP

THE COSTUME

'Dressing Up' is as important in the kitchen as it is on stage. If a dancer's costume is not right for the part, then all is lost, and so it is with food — a dish can be made or marred by its final 'dressing'. Too much, or too little, is critical.

These comparisons with stage terms, that have a similar application to cooking, forge the link between the two arts, such worlds apart in the visual sense, but closely linked in universal appreciation.

Modern dance is a seeking for individual expression. 'dressing up food'can be an equal expression.

Garnishes, sauces, creams and dressings all play their part in the Finale, complimented by the carefully selected serving dishes, which need not mean expensive china, plain white, old junk shop china, paper or whatever — it is the compatability with the food that counts — one wouldn't put a steak & kidney pudding on fine bone china, or delicate Pavlova on earthenware!

Presentation gives pleasure to the one preparing, and incomparable delight to those fortunate enough to be partaking. The reward to the performer on stage is a FULL HOUSE, to the chef or cook it is an EMPTY PLATE.

NOTES

There are no hard and fast rules as to which vinegar and oils one uses for dressings, or to quantities.

Generally proportions for vinaigrette are 3 parts oil to 1 part vinegar.

OILS

Olive Oil: Stores well in a cool place.
Olives are easy to press, releasing their oil without the need of heat, therefore contain fewer impurities than most vegetable oils.
Vitamins A, D, E & K.

Virgin Oil: Sometimes called Lucca Oil or Green Oil.
Virgin oil is the first pressing of the olives, producing the best oil — may have a greenish tinge.

Corn Oil or Maize Oil: Stores well in a cool place.
The oil is separated from the grain by centrifugal force using water.
Vitamins A, D, & E.

Sesame Oil: Stores well even in warm conditions, does not go rancid.
The top grade is golden in colour, coming from the first seed pressings. Next grade is darker in colour, made under hydraulic pressure, inferior to first grade.

Sunflower Oil: Stores well.
Almost half the sunflower seed is made up of oil, usually extracted by pressing.
Vitamins A, D & E.

Ground Nut Oil: Stores well at room temperature.
Mostly extracted by cold pressings, a cheaper way is to use chemical solvents. The oil is then refined, heated and treated with antioxidents.
Vitamins & Minerals.

Vinegars

Cider Vinegar, Wine Vinegar, Tarragon Vinegar

Methods

Vinaigrettes

Use an electric Blender, or screw top jar.

Ingredients do not actually blend, need shaking frequently, and again before serving.

Stores well.

Use for salads, pasta dishes, meats, raw vegetables.

Mayonnaise

Use electric blender, or bowl and whisk.

These need VERY careful mixing. The important part is adding the oil to the egg mixture, a little at a time, dripped in until the mayonnaise is smooth and creamy. Should the mixture curdle, beat another egg in a clean bowl, and gradually stir into curdled mixture. Olive oil is generally used but if a lighter taste is preferred use one of the other oils.

Butters

1. Butter should be softened, though not melted.
2. Chop herbs, garlic, parsley & lemon (Maître d'Hôtel) or any other desired flavour.
3. Add these, plus seasoning to taste, to the butter. Mix well.
4. Put butter on to a piece off greaseproof paper or foil, roll up into a sausage shape about 2.5cm/1″ diameter. Place in fridge until cold.
5. When cold and before serving cut into slices about 1.25cm/½″ thick.

Delicious served on grilled meat or fish, in baked potatoes or in hot french bread.

Sauces — Sweet & Savoury

Basic proportion 50g/2oz butter, 50g/2oz flour = 100g/4oz roux.

A sauce not only enhances the flavour of the food but transforms an ordinary dish to something special, (and can very often cover a multitude of sins).

Sauces take careful preparation and you must give them your full attention whilst cooking. This does not mean they take a long time or are involved — this is not so. They are quick to prepare, but 'staying with them' during cooking brings its rewards.

Garnishes

Lemons, parsley, chives, mushrooms, tomatoes, rosemary, mint, etc. Nuts, seeds, muesli,'caramelized sugar, chocolate.

Individual expression here again as to whether you slice, twist, grate, chop, leave whole, mix, or use alone, imagination, artistry.

You have the materials, now you create the costume.

Vinaigrette Dressing

1 tbsp vinegar, cider or wine
3 tbsp oil
Pinch of mustard powder
Pinch of paprika

Method

Put vinegar into a screw topped jar, add mustard and paprika, shake well.

Now add oil, shake well again.

This can be used as it is, or variations added to it. Always shake well before use.

French Dressing

6 tbsp olive oil
2 tbsp white wine vinegar
½ level teaspoon french mustard
1 clove garlic peeled & crushed
Salt & black pepper to taste

Method

Place all ingredients into a screw topped jar and shake well until all ingredients are combined.
Shake again before serving. Keeps well.

Mayonnaise

2 egg yolks (at room temperature)
280ml/ ½ pint oil (mixed olive & sunflower best, but can be either)
2 tbsp white wine vinegar
pinch mustard powder
Salt & black pepper

Method

Either use an electric blender or bowl and whisk. (See notes at front of section).

1. Beat egg yolks with the mustard, salt & pepper.
2. Add oil a drop at a time until half is used, whisking constantly until thickened, add 1 tbsp of the wine at this point, then rest of oil, very slowly
3. Now add rest of vinegar. If too thick a teaspoon of boiling water can be added.

Garlic Mayonnaise (sometimes called Aioli)
Make as for basic mayonnaise adding at beginning 2 cloves of garlic, crushed.

Avocado Mayonnaise
Peel and stone 1 avocado, mash well, add to egg yolks at beginning — make as mayonnaise.

Yogurt Mayonnaise

125g/5oz natural yogurt
1 tbsp sunflower or olive oil
2 tsp white wine vinegar
1 tsp whole grain mustard

Method

Mix all ingredients together. Chill well before serving.

Cream Mayonnaise

Mix together equal parts made mayonnaise with sour cream or fresh double cream. Stir well. Chill.

Honey & Yogurt Dressing

125ml/5oz natural yogurt
1 tsp clear honey
1 tbsp mayonnaise
1 tsp lemon juice

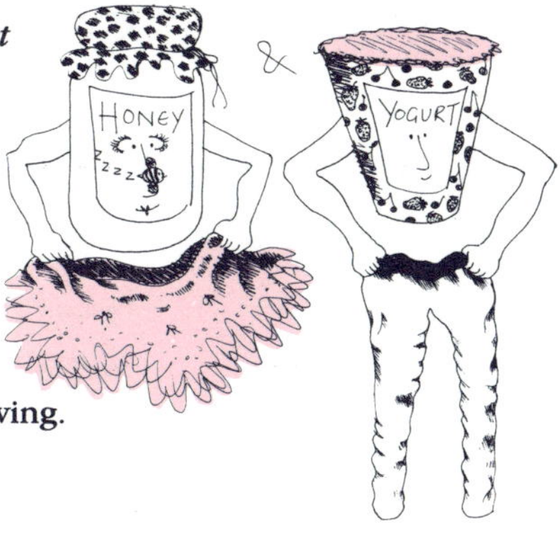

Method

Mix all ingredients together, chill before serving.

Savoury Butters

Maître d'Hôtel

100g/4oz butter
2 tbsp fresh chopped parsley
1 tsp lemon juice
Salt & ground black pepper

Prepare as for savoury butters.
Serve with fish or meat.

Garlic Butter

100g/4oz butter
2 cloves garlic, crushed

Mix as for savoury butter.
One can add many variations of flavours to butter, i.e. curry, tomato purée, shrimps, herbs.

SAVOURY SAUCES

Basic White Sauce

25g/1oz flour
25g/1oz butter
570ml/1 pint milk
¼ tsp salt
Black pepper

These quantities can be halved if only requiring 200ml/½ pint.

Method

1. Melt butter in saucepan.
2. Add flour, stir over a low heat using wooden spoon for about 2 minutes. Do not allow mixture to brown.
3. Remove pan from heat, gradually blend in the milk, stirring continually to prevent lumps, and continue to cook until sauce thickens.
4. Simmer gently for a further 2 - 3 minutes. Add seasoning.

Quick White Sauce

Not technically correct, but I find very quick and useful, and never fails.

280ml/½ pint milk
25g/1oz flour
25g/1oz butter
Pepper & salt

Method

1. Put butter in saucepan and melt.
2. Blend the flour with a little of the milk until smooth paste, then stir in rest of milk until smooth.
3. Add to butter in saucepan, stir continually over medium heat until sauce thickens. Stir for 2 - 3 minutes. Add seasoning.

Add grated cheese, chopped sauté onion, or chopped parsley to the above basic sauces depending on the type of sauce required.

Hollandaise Sauce

1 tsp lemon juice
1 tsp wine vinegar
4 egg yolks
Small bay leaf
200g/8oz butter
Salt & fresh ground pepper

Method

1. Put lemon juice, vinegar and bay leaf into saucepan and simmer gently for a few minutes.
2. Put beaten egg yolks into a bowl, standing over a saucepan of boiling water (or use double saucepan). Add lemon & vinegar mix after removing bay leaf. Whisk until mixture thickens.
3. Gradually add butter, stirring continually. Season with salt & pepper.

Serve with fish, eggs, chicken and vegetable dishes.

Horseradish Sauce

140ml/5oz soured cream or fresh cream
4 tbps horseradish relish
½ tsp worcester sauce

Method

Mix all ingredients together until blended.
Serve with roast beef or mackerel.

Bread Sauce

1 onion
280ml/½ pint milk
75g/3oz fresh white breadcrumbs
1 bay leaf
25g/1oz butter
2 cloves
Salt & white pepper

Method

1. Stick cloves into peeled onion, place in a saucepan with the milk and bay leaf, bring to boil, remove from heat. Leave standing for 10 minutes, then remove onion, cloves and bay leaf.
2. Add breadcrumbs and seasoning to milk and return to heat. Simmer gently for 10 minutes, add butter. If too thick add a little more milk or cream, if too thin add more breadcrumbs.

Serve with turkey, chicken or pheasant.

Apple Sauce

400g/1lb cooking apples
3 tbsp water
12g/½oz butter – optional

Method

1. Peel, core and slice apples. Place in saucepan with water.
2. Cook gently until a pulp, leave to cool, sieve or mash to a purée, add butter if liked.

Serve with roast pork or pork chops.

Mint Sauce

Large bunch mint
1 tsp sugar
2 tbsp boiling water
4 tbsp vinegar, either wine or malt

Method

1. Remove leaves from mint, wash, dry, then chop finely, with knife or cut with scissors, or in food blender.
2. Put mint into a bowl with the sugar, add boiling water, this is to melt the sugar and bring out the flavour of the mint. Now add vinegar.

Serve with roast lamb or lamb chops.
If you put this sauce in a screw topped jar it keeps for weeks. I always make enough in the summer to last all winter.

SWEET SAUCES AND BUTTERS

Basic White Sauce (sweet)

1 tbsp cornflour
25g/1oz caster sugar
12g/½oz butter
280ml/½ pint milk
Vanilla essence

Method

1. Blend the cornflour with a little cold milk.
2. Bring rest of milk to boil, pour on to cornflour, stirring all the time.
3. Return to saucepan, with the butter and sugar. Continue to stir until thickened and smooth.
4. Add 2 or 3 drops of vanilla essence.

One can add your own flavourings to the above sauce, chopped nuts, dried fruit, chocolate chips, etc.

Chantilly Cream

140ml/¼ pint fresh double cream
½ an egg white
12g/½oz icing sugar
Vanilla flavouring

Method

1. Whisk cream until thick and holds its peaks.
2. whisk egg white until thick, fold into cream.
3. Add icing sugar and 2 or 3 drops vanilla. Fold in.

Chill before serving.
Serve with summer pudding, fruit salads, chocolate puddings and cakes!

Brandy Butter

100g/4oz unsalted butter, softened but not melted
100g/4oz icing sugar, sifted
100g/4oz caster sugar
1 tbsp brandy

Method

1. Beat butter until creamy.
2. Beat in gradually icing and caster sugars, adding brandy in between. Beat until smooth. (A drop of cream or milk can be added if too thick).
3. Put into serving dish. Leave to harden in fridge.

Traditionally served with Christmas pudding, but lovely any time.

Chocolate Nut Butter

100g/4oz unsalted butter, softened but not melted
2 tsp caster sugar
1 tbsp plain grated chocolate
1 tbsp chopped hazelnuts (or walnuts)

Method

Beat butter until smooth and creamy, add sugar, chocolate and nuts. Nice and crunchy. Put in serving dish, leave to harden in fridge.
Serve with hot puddings and pastries.

Butterscotch Sauce

2 tbsp golden syrup
25g/1oz butter
75g/3oz brown sugar
1 ½ tbsp cornflour
280ml/10 fl.oz (½ pint) water

Method

1. Put syrup, butter and sugar in a pan and cook until sugar begins to caramelize.
2. Mix cornflour with a little water, then add the rest.
3. Remove syrup from heat and add cornflour. Return to the heat and cook until thickened.

Chocolate Sauce

75g/3oz plain chocolate
100g/4oz caster or soft brown sugar
1 small tin evaporated milk
⅛ tsp cream of tartar
1 tbsp vanilla essence
Pinch salt

Method

1. Melt the chocolate in a bowl over a pan of simmering water.
2. When cooled a little add cream of tartar, salt and sugar and mix well.
3. Blend in the milk, return the sauce to the pan and cook slowly over a low heat until the sauce thickens.
4. Remove from the heat and add the vanilla.

You can use orange flavoured chocolate and 1 tbsp orange flavoured liquor, or After Eight mints and 1 tbsp crème de menthe.

Nice served with anything! Hot or cold.

Chocolate Fudge Sauce

70ml/2½oz single cream
25g/1oz cocoa powder
100g/4oz caster sugar
150g/6oz golden syrup
25g/1oz butter
½ tsp vanilla essence or sugar

Method

1. Put all ingredients except vanilla into a saucepan and mix well.
2. Bring slowly to boil, stirring to avoid sticking. Boil for 5 minutes, add vanilla.
3. Cool sauce before serving.

Chocolate Rum Sauce

200g/8oz plain chocolate
50g/2oz butter
4 tbsp milk
2 tbsp rum

Method

1. Break chocolate into small pieces and place in a bowl over pan of hot water until chocolate has melted.
2. Add butter, milk and rum, stirring occasionally until smooth and glossy.

Melba Sauce

400g/1lb fresh or frozen raspberries
1 level tbsp cornflour
1 tbsp water 50g/2oz caster sugar
Grated rind & juice of 1 lemon

Quantities can be halved

Method

1. Remove stalk from raspberries, cook with water over gently heat for 10 - 15 minutes, until reduced to a pulp.
2. Remove from heat, pass through a sieve.
3. Blend cornflour and a small drop of water to a cream. Stir into the fruit purée.
4. Return to saucepan, stir over low heat until thickened (1 - 2 minutes).
5. Add sugar, lemon juice and rind.
6. Cool.

Serve with peaches & icecream.

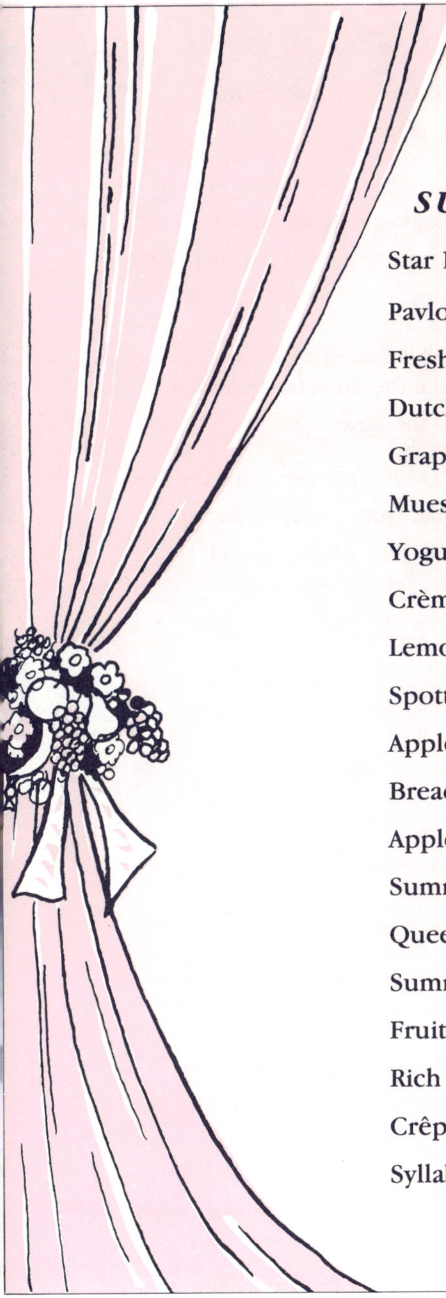

ACT 2

SCENE 3

SUGAR PLUM PUDS

STAR BILLING

'Pavlova's' name again. How fitting that such a light, delicious sweet should be so named.

Well, you all have your chance, fame is either with you, or ahead of you, so who can tell. Maybe in the future such a comparison will be made with your name in another recipe book.

I have mixed good old fashioned puddings with contemporary desserts, for, like the movements in dance, the old still finds a place with the new.

As you aim for a star, so the 'Dining Dancer' aims for the pudding at the end of the meal, with anticipation and pleasure, keeping the best until last. Enjoy yourself.

Pavlova

3 egg whites
200g/8oz caster sugar
pinch of salt
1 tsp vanilla essence
1 tsp vinegar (ordinary malt vinegar)
1 tsp cornflour
280mls/½ pint double cream
raspberries, strawberries, bananas, kiwi fruit as in season or preference — a mixed pavlova is lovely.

Oven: Gas no 1. 275°F. 140°C. 1 hour
Baking sheet, greaseproof paper

Method

1. Draw a circle 23cm/9″ on non-stick or greaseproof paper and place on baking sheet.
2. Whisk egg whites with pinch of salt until very stiff.

3. Mix cornflour with sugar and gradually add to egg whites, whisking to keep stiff.
4. Fold in the vanilla and vinegar.
5. Spread mixture over the circle, try to make the outside edge slightly higher than the centre, or pipe meringue round edge of circle to give an edge.
6. Place in oven. When cooked (should be firm) remove, leave to cool, then carefully slide on to serving plate.

Note: If you want to keep the meringue case, put in airtight tin until needed.
7. Whip double cream, fill centre of meringue case, arrange fruit of choice on top of cream — being generous and artistic.

Fresh Fruit Torte — no cooking

100g/4oz shortbread fingers or Nice biscuits
75g/3oz caster sugar
75g/3oz unsalted butter
1 egg — beaten
280mls/½ pint double cream
1 tsp icing sugar
300g/12oz strawberries, or raspberries, grapes, cherries, pineapple (cleaned & chopped)

800g/2lb loaf tin — lined with greaseproof paper

Method

1. Place biscuits in polythene bag and crush till fine using a rolling pin. Put half the crushed biscuits into the lined loaf tin and press firmly over base.
2. Cream butter and sugar until light and fluffy. Beat in egg and when blended spoon over biscuit base.
3. Whip cream until thick with the icing sugar.

4. Put layer of cream, then layer of chopped fruit. Repeat again, finishing with cream.
5. Cover cream with remaining crushed biscuits. Cover with clingfilm, put to freeze for 24 hours.

After removing from freezer leave at room temperature for approx 1 hour. Turn onto serving plate, decorate with fruit or nuts.
You can make this without using a freezer, just in fridge, though it isn't so firm or easy to cut. Tastes delicious though. Do NOT store in freezer, it does not keep long term.

Dutch Delight

2 cartons (280mls/½ pint) soured cream
1 tbsp sweet sherry
1 tbsp clear honey
200g/½lb green grapes, de-stalked, left whole

Method

1. Beat the sherry and honey into the soured cream, add the grapes.
2. Put into serving dish or individual dishes. Serve chilled with biscuit fingers. Lovely and refreshing.

Grape & Nut Grill

280mls/½ pint double cream
2 cartons (small) natural yogurt
4 tbsp demerara sugar
50g/2oz chopped hazelnuts
200g/1lb black grapes, de-stalked & de-seeded

Method

1. Beat double cream until thick.
2. Fold in the natural yogurt and chopped nuts, then the grapes.
3. Put into ovenproof dish, sprinkle with the demerara sugar.
4. Put under hot grill until sugar bubbles — serve at once.

Easy to prepare, easy to eat!

Muesli Magic

100g/4oz muesli
1 carton plain (or fruit) yogurt
1 block ice cream
25g/1oz flaked chocolate

Method

1. Put muesli into grill pan. Put under hot grill, shaking to prevent burning, until crispy. Remove and put to cool.
2. Place icecream block on serving dish and tip yogurt over the top.
3. Cover top and sides of icecream with cooled crispy muesli.
4. Sprinkle chocolate flakes on top.

Serve at once.

You can do this so easily for just 1, with a single ice cream, and a little muesli.

Yogurt

570mls/1 pint fresh milk
3 tsp natural yogurt
Vacuum flask or yogurt maker

Method

1. Bring milk to boiling point, boil for 1 - 2 minutes on very low heat — move saucepan from side to side to prevent boiling over. Cool.
2. Cool milk to 43°C (110°F) using a thermometer. If you haven't one, test by putting in your finger — should be just comfortably warm
3. Stir in the yogurt, mixing well. Put mixture into vacuum flask or yogurt maker, leave for 5 - 10 hours (or cover with clingfilm and leave in a warm place).
4. When set, stir the yogurt, then put to chill in fridge. Chilling stops the bacteria working.

You can add fresh fruit to your yogurt, or honey & nuts, muesli, or eat it plain. Use to add to other dishes.
Keep 2 - 3 tablespoonfuls of yogurt to make your next lot.

Crème Brulée

570mls/1 pint fresh whipping cream
4 egg yolks
75g/3oz caster sugar
1 tsp. vanilla flavouring
(ingredients can be halved)

Oven: Gas no. 2. 300°F. 150°C. 1 hour
6 ramekin dishes

Method

1. Put cream into a bowl over a pan of hot water, or in a double saucepan. Heat gently, do not boil.
2. Place egg yolks and 50g/2oz of the sugar in a bowl, beat well, add vanilla essence.
3. Pour on fresh cream to egg mixture, whisk thoroughly.
4. Pour into individual dishes. Place dishes in a meat tin with water in the tin coming half way up ramekin dishes. Put in oven. Bake 1 hour until set, remove and leave till cold.
5. Leave in fridge, preferably overnight. Just before serving, sprinkle remaining sugar over the top of each créme brulée, put under hot grill until sugar turns brown.

Small pyrex dishes can be used — as long as they stand heat of grill.
This is a delicious sweet, well worth making.

Lemon Fluff

570mls/1 pint milk
2 eggs, separated
100g/4oz sugar
50g/2oz soft margarine
50g/2oz S.R. flour
2 lemons

Oven: Gas no. 5. 375°F. 190°C.
40 - 50 minutes
Buttered ovenproof dish.

Method

1. Cream together margarine and sugar. Add egg yolks.
2. Stir in flour and a little of the milk — to make a smooth paste.
3. Grate lemons and squeeze juice.
4. Add rest of milk to mixture, plus lemon rind and lemon juice. It will look very runny and curdled.
5. Whisk egg whites till stiff. Fold gently into mixture.
6. Pour into prepared dish, place dish in baking tin with cold water coming half way up dish. This keeps pudding moist. Place in oven.

Lovely hot or cold — don't scrimp on the lemons — it needs a sharp taste.

Spotted Dick (Roly Poly) For Giles

200g/8oz S.R. four
50g/2oz soft breadcrumbs
100g/4oz shredded suet
150g/6oz currants
water to mix
pudding cloth or clean tea towel

Method

1. Put flour, breadcrumbs and suet in a bowl, mix together.
2. Wash currants and dry — add to flour.
3. Mix with water using a knife until mixture comes together in a soft dough.
4. Turn onto floured board and shape into a roll.
5. Put onto pudding cloth, fold over cloth, either tie ends with string, or use safety pin.
6. Bring water to boil in large saucepan. Immerse pudding into water, and when boiling reduce heat. Keep simmering for 2 hours.

cont/...

7. Drain water, lift out pudding, untie cloth and put onto serving plate.

Serve with butter and brown sugar for people to help themselves to.

Apple Fritters

400g/1lb cooking apples, peeled and cored (can use eating apples)
1 tsp lemon juice — optional
vegetable oil for cooking
100g/4oz plain flour
2 eggs
2 tbsp milk
pinch salt
caster sugar for serving

Method

1. Peel & core apples. Cut into thick slices 6mm/1/4", put on kitchen paper to dry, then sprinkle with lemon juice if using.
2. Put flour & salt into a bowl, add eggs, whisk until smooth. Now add milk, using a little extra if too thick — should be a thick runny consistency.
3. Put sliced apples into batter.
4. Heat oil in pan. When very hot put apple slices dipped in batter into pan. Cook quickly a few minutes each side till golden brown. Remove with a slice and put on kitchen paper to drain. Keep warm. Serve dusted with caster sugar.

You can use bananas, peaches, pineapple for fritters, also jam sandwiches — make in usual way cutting off crusts and making suitable size. Dip in batter and fry.

Bread Pudding

1 large loaf white or brown
approx. 570mls/1 pint water
100g/4oz shredded suet
2 eggs
200g/8oz mixed fruit (currants, sultanas, raisins)
50g/2oz brown sugar
2 tsp mixed spice

Oven: Gas no: 5. 350°F. 190°C. 1¼ hrs.
Ovenproof buttered dish or meat dish.

Method

1. Break bread into pieces, put in bowl, cover with the water. Leave to soak for 10 minutes.
2. Drain any surplus water from bread, either by putting in a colander or squeezing with hands.
3. In basin put soaked bread, suet, mixed spice, sugar, dried fruit and eggs. Mix all together using a fork.
4. Turn into a greased dish, put in oven. Serve hot sprinkled with sugar or cut when cold.

Note
If rather wet, add a tbsp of flour to mixture.

Apple (or other fruit) Crumble

Filling

400g/1lb cooking apples, or blackberries & apple, gooseberries, rhubarb, plums, apricots, etc.
25g/1oz butter
100g/4oz sugar — white or brown
pinch of cinnamon (optional if not wanting spicy taste)
2 - 3 tbsp water

Topping

75g/3oz butter or margarine
50g/2oz brown or white sugar
150g/6oz brown or white flour

Oven: Gas no: 4. 350°F. 180°C. 45 minutes
Buttered ovenproof dish

Method

1. Peel, core and slice apples (or top & tail gooseberries, halve plums and apricots, de-stalk blackberries).
2. Put fruit into dish, sprinkle with the sugar and cinnamon, put in water (enough to moisten fruit) and dot with butter.
3. Put flour and fat in bowl, rub fat into flour, add sugar. Mix to a breadcrumb type of consistency.
4. Sprinkle this mixture over fruit. Bake in oven till golden brown.

Summer Pudding

600g/1½lb soft fruit, i.e. raspberries, strawberries, blackberries, redcurrants or mixed.
5 or 6 slices bread
100g/4oz soft brown sugar
1.25 litres/2 pint pudding basin

Method

1. Put fruit, sugar and a small amount of water into saucepan. Heat slowly till sugar dissolves. Simmer 5 - 6 minutes, remove from heat.
2. Cut crusts from bread, cut into fingers, line the base and sides of basin with bread.
3. Gently pour in half the fruit.
4. Put a layer of bread on top of fruit.
5. Pour in half remaining fruit.
6. Layer of bread on — then rest of fruit.
7. Press top down with a saucer and put a weight on the saucer (which serves to press the fruit & bread together well.) Leave pudding overnight, or few hours in fridge till really cold. I usually stand basin on a plate in case juice leaks.
8. When cold, turn pudding out, upside down onto a plate. Decorate with fruit on top and round edges.

Serve with cream, ice cream or plain yogurt.

Really delicious.

Queen of Puddings

75g/3oz soft white breadcrumbs
420mls/ 3⁄4 pint milk
25g/1oz butter
75g/3oz caster sugar
2 eggs — separated
2 tsp grated lemon or orange rind
2 tbsp red jam

Oven: Gas no. 3. 325°F. 170°C. 40 minutes
Buttered ovenproof dish

Method

1. Warm the milk with the butter and lemon or orange rind. Do not boil.
2. Stir 25g/1oz sugar into the egg yolks and pour warmed milk onto yolks.
3. Add crumbs to this mixture, stir well, pour into greased pie dish. Leave to stand for half an hour.
4. Put in oven, bake 40 minutes.
5. Remove pudding from oven and reduce heat to Gas 1 or 2. 250°F. 130°C.
6. Whisk egg whites till stiff and fold in remaining sugar.
7. Spread jam over top of pudding, spoon meringue over jam. Return to oven for approx. 40 minutes till meringue is set and golden brown.

Serve hot.

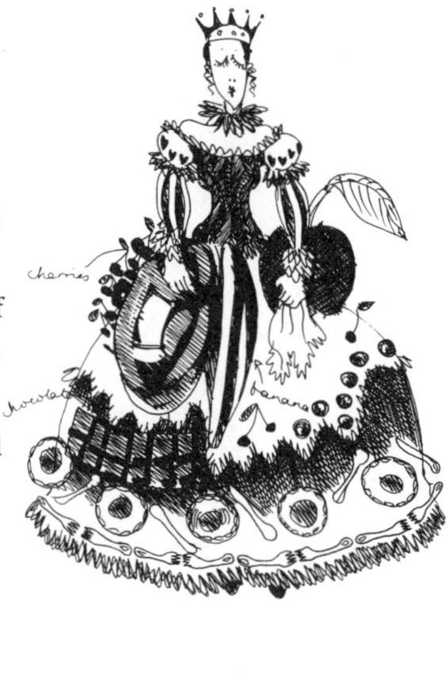

Summer Crêpes

Batter

100g/4oz plain flour
pinch salt
1 egg plus 1 egg yolk
1 tbsp oil or melted butter
280ml/½ pint milk

Makes about 10 crêpes

Filling

200g/8oz soft fruit — raspberries, strawberries or tin of strained fruit — mandarins or peaches, etc.
140mls/5oz double cream
tsp honey
icing sugar to dust

Method

1. Sieve flour and salt into a basin, make a hollow in the middle, put in the egg plus extra egg yolk, the melted butter or oil, and half the milk. Gradually draw in the flour from the sides using a wooden spoon, till all flour is incorporated. Add remaining milk and beat till smooth. Note — or use Food Mixer.
2. Pour batter into a jug for ease of use.
3. Crêpes should be cooked in a really hot pan that has only been greased with oil — not have any running — re-grease between each crêpe.
4. Pour 2 tbsp approx. of batter into hot pan, tilt it so that batter runs to edges and cook till golden brown underneath — either turn, or toss, and cook other side. Continue till all batter is used.
5. Keep crêpes warm either on a plate over pan of boiling water or in a warming oven, covered with foil.

cont/...

6. Filling — Beat cream till thick, fold in honey and fresh fruit — keep cold till ready to put in crêpes.
7. To Serve — put a spoonful of cream mixture into each crêpe, fold over in half, dust with icing sugar.

Fruit Fool 1

400g/1lb gooseberries (you can use plums, apricots, etc.)
100g/4oz sugar
water to cook
570mls/1 pint made thick custard, using 570mls/1 pint milk

Method

1. Make custard in normal way. Put to cool — cover top so skin does not form.
2. Prepare & wash fruit, put with sugar in saucepan and cook till soft and pulpy (do not burn) — (only enough water to cover bottom of pan).
3. When fruit is cool, put into liquidizer and liquidize to a smooth purée, or pass through a sieve.
4. Put fruit into a bowl, add made custard. Whisk well together till thick creamy consistency.
5. Place in individual dishes or large serving bowl — put in fridge till cold.

Decorate with fresh fruit.

Special Fruit Fool 2

300g/ 3/4lb fresh raspberries or strawberries
1 tbsp caster sugar
280mls/½ pint double cream
fruit to decorate

Method

1. Rub washed fruit through a sieve or liquidise. Add sugar to taste.
2. Beat double cream till thick and holding peaks.
3. Fold fruit into cream till well blended.
4. Put into individual dishes, decorate with whole fruit — cool in fridge for at least 2 hours.

Rich Trifle

400g/1lb fresh raspberries (or any soft fruit)
125g/5oz caster sugar
8 trifle sponges
2 tbsp raspberry or strawberry jam
4 tbsp sherry
1 pint custard (using custard powder)
280ml/½ pint double cream
25g/1oz toasted almonds
Chocolate flakes to decorate

Method

1. Put fruit into a bowl, reserving a few to decorate the top. Sprinkle with the sugar and leave for 1 hour until the juices run.
2. Cut sponges in half, spread with jam. Sandwich together, place in bottom of dish.
3. Spoon sherry over the sponges.
4. Now put fruit over the sponges & the juice.
5. If wanting an extra rich trifle you can now put a layer of different fruit, i.e. peaches.
6. Make up custard, leave to cool for about 20 minutes, and pour on top of sponge mixture.
7. Whip double cream, pipe or spoon top of custard attractively.

8. Decorate with almonds, or chocolate flakes and remainder of fresh fruit.
9. Keep chilled.

Crêpe Suzette (need 2 per person, recipe makes 12)

Batter

100g/4oz plain flour — pinch salt
1 egg & 1 egg yolk
1 tbsp melted butter or oil
280ml/½ pint milk

Orange Butter

100g/4oz unsalted butter
100g/4oz caster sugar
Finely grated rind 2 oranges
Juice of 1 orange
2 tbsp Grand Marnier liqueur

Method

Crêpes

1. Sieve flour into basin with salt, make well in centre.
2. Put egg & extra egg yolk, plus melted butter or oil into centre of flour, and half the milk, draw the flour into the liquid with a wooden spoon, beat well with spoon.
3. Stir in the remaining milk.

Note: One can of course use an electric mixer if preferred.

Cooking crêpes

4. Get pan really hot, having coated it with butter or oil by wiping it round with kitchen paper — do not have any running fat.
5. Pour 2 tbsp batter into pan, tilt each way so bottom is coated and cook until underside is golden (1 minute). Toss, or turn with slice. Cook other side, remove and put on warm plate, cover, and put over saucepan of hot water or in warm oven.

6. Reheat pan, continue procedure until all crêpes are cooked.

Orange Butter

7. Cream butter and sugar until light.
8. Add grated orange rind, then slowly beat in the juice and liqueur.

Crêpe Suzette

9. Melt a little orange butter in pan.
10. Drop one cooked crêpe into butter, baste, fold in 3 – push to one side.
11. Continue this way, adding a little orange butter before each crêpe, until they are all cooked – if pan is not big enough put into heatproof serving dish, keeping warm in oven.
12. When serving, add a little more liqueur or brandy, and set light. (This should be done at the table).

Lovely served with double cream. I use a zester to get rind from an orange and sprinkle this on top of the crêpes.

Syllabub (serves 6)

2 medium sized lemons
6 tbsp sweet sherry
75g/3oz caster sugar
420g/$^{3}/_{4}$ pint double cream

Method

1. Grate lemon rind finely, squeeze juice into container.
2. Whisk cream until thick and holding peaks.
3. Combine lemon juice, rind, sherry and sugar in a bowl. Stir until sugar is dissolved.
4. Add cream, whisk again until thick.
5. Spoon into individual glasses, put to chill.

Decorate with zest of lemon rind, or thin slices of lemon.

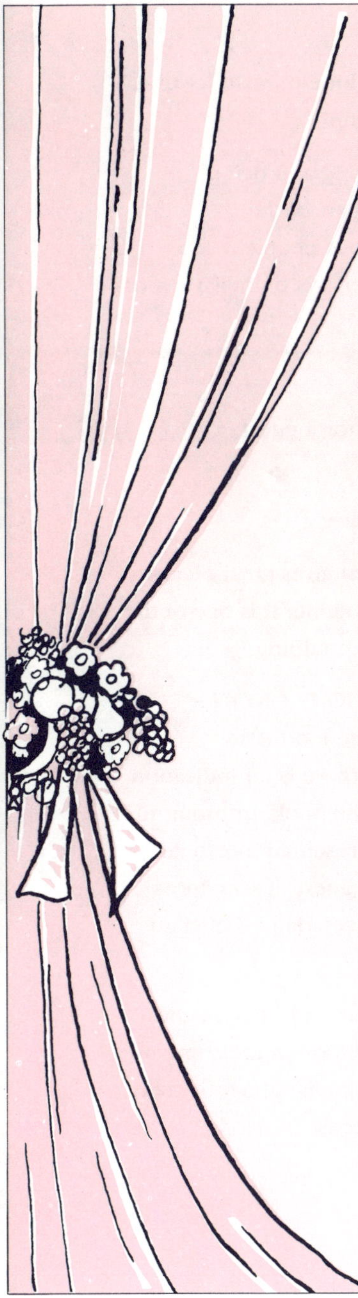

ACT 2

SCENE 4

ENTERTAINERS

ON WITH THE SHOW

GRACE "In a hungry and sometimes lonely world let us give thanks for this food and fellowship"

Show people generally love entertaining and being entertained, especially when food is part of the programme. Being hospitable, generous people themselves, they fully appreciate the efforts of their Host or Hostess.

Entertaining, definition being:-

'Hospitality at table, accommodation for a guest, a Banquet'.

What more could one ask for, or receive.

Planning, preparing and serving a meal gives great pleasure to the one preparing and the one indulging. It is one of the oldest and most universal ways of entertaining.

In this section I have given SUGGESTIONS ONLY for various types of Menus. Sometimes the food is self explanatory, i.e. Smoked Salmon, or there is an indication as to where suggested dishes are in the book. Impromptu, or a planned meal — remember — presentation can add much to the pleasure. Consider your guest, if you know they have a weight problem or are vegetarian — cater to those needs.

I have gone from Kitchen Tea to Caviar and Champagne — the secret is in the enjoyment of good food in the company of good friends. If, of course, the setting is Romantic then an audience of one is all the show needs!

SETTING THE SCENE

If a Romantic Meal for two is called for then soft lights, roses, a simple meal is all that is required! Let Cupid do the rest.

DINNERS If semi-formal are a golden opportunity to "set the table" and the atmosphere. Try picking a colour, a theme, and carrying it through to even the small details, i.e. Mediaeval — straw on floor, platters for food used for each reserve (serving), clay pipes for the men, spices to smell for ladies, peasants sat at end of table. Minstrel playing (or tape of Mediaeval Music) Mead and Rough Wine to drink.

OR — Black & White — Food, table settings, invite cards and menus, all as near black and white as you can get. Place mats can be made from black and white paper or card. Black and White Minstrel music. Guests to dress in Black and White.

OR — Odds and Ends — Use all odd china and cutlery, odds and ends of food, even mis-match the guests.

OR 1920 or 1930s Elegant Meal

Decide on the theme, start from the beginning with the invitations, then build up the ideas from then. Great Fun. Parties are also fun with a theme, i.e. School Days, Tramps and Toffs, Masked, T.V. Characters, Nursery Rhyme.

CHOCOLATE FREAKS MENU

"Not for Slimmers"

CHOCOLATE PATÉ

(Scene 5, page 189)

CHOCOLATE OMELETTE

(Scene 5, page 190)

CHOCOLATE SALAD

(Scene 5, page 191)

CHOCOLATE ROMANCE

(Scene 5, page 199)

DRINKING CHOCOLATE

with

CHOCOLATE SHORTBREAD

(Scene 5, page 192)

CURACAO LIQUEUR

BRUNCH

Usually served between 11am — 3pm, a cross between breakfast and lunch. Can be very simple or extravagant to celebrate a special occasion or an excuse to sit lazily with friends without overeating or drinking, yet feeling rather decadent.

Food should be kept light and guests help themselves — Wine or Champagne only, not beers or spirits.

SUGGESTED MENUS

Smoked Salmon & Scrambled Eggs — 50g/2oz Salmon per person — 2 eggs per person.
Strawberries & Cream
Selection of Soft Cheeses
Hot Brown Rolls and Butter

"Champagne"
Fresh Fruit Juice
Coffee

1. Salmon served on bed of lettuce, with lemon wedges.
2. Scrambled Eggs in warm dish, trail cream on top.
3. Strawberries in a glass dish, set on bed of crushed ice, accompanied by bowl of whipped double cream and caster sugar.

OR

Large platter of thinly sliced Ham and breast of Chicken
Plate of Melon Slices and Grapes
Gooseberry Crumble and Cream
Selection of Soft Cheeses
French Bread and Butter
Iced Sparkling Wine
Fresh Fruit Drinks
Coffee

KITCHEN BRUNCH

Once again, let guests help themselves — just make sure there is plenty of hot coffee, bread and cheeses.

SUGGESTED DISHES

Kedgeree, garnished with fresh cream and parsley (p.56)
Waffles with honey or maple syrup
Selection of Soft Cheeses, Ryvita and Rye Bread
Wine
Fruit Juice
Coffee

OR

Grilled Bacon, Eggs, Mushrooms
Fresh Fruit and Yogurt
Selection of Soft Cheeses
French Bread
Fresh Fruit Juice
Coffee

Bought waffles are very good if you do not want to make your own. They take 2 - 3 minutes to heat under the grill.

OR

Omelettes — have various fillings prepared — guests make a filling of their own
Selection of Salads
Fruit Cake (p.112)
Cheeseboard & Biscuits
Fruit Juices
Coffee

LUNCH

Can be served at table, or as a lap lunch. Consider ease of eating if friends are to use one hand to hold their plate and one for drinks! If guests are vegetarian or slimming take that into account before deciding what to serve.

Suggestions for "Sit at Table Lunch"

1. Pork or Veal Escalopes in Orange (p.47)
   New Potatoes with butter and mint
   Selection of Salads and Dressings

   Chocolate Pots (p.22)

   Cheeseboard and Biscuits

   Wine — Coffee

OR

2. Chicken Madeira (p.180)
   Sauté Potatoes
   Broccoli and Courgettes

   Summer Pudding (p.160)

   Cheeseboard and Biscuits

   Wine — Coffee

VEGETARIAN LUNCH

Courgettes à la Provençale (p.79)
Stir Fry Bean Shoots

Apple Cake and Cream (p.99)

Cheeseboard and Biscuits

Fruit Juice

Coffee

LAP LUNCHES

1. Lasagne (p.181)
   Green Salad

   Apricot Fool (p.128)
   Honey Squares (p.105)

   Wine and Coffee

2. Cottage Pie (p.37)
   Carrots and Runner Beans

   Cheesecake or Lemon Fluff (p.101 & p.155)

   Wine, Coffee

As long as the meal is balanced in its content then the choice is a personal one.

AFTERNOON TEA

How typically English this sounds, but how delightful conjuring up a picture of tea on the lawn, gracious ladies and the sound of the croquet balls being gently knocked. You too can re-create the essence of that period. Pretty china, a cloth and napkins, dainty food, can have a very relaxing effect, though of course the alternative of a hot cup of tea and a heart to heart with a friend over the kitchen table is the back bone of England.

'TEA IS SERVED' Suggestions

Very thin, dainty sandwiches of:-

Thin Cucumber or Tomato, Egg and Cress, Salmon, Paste. Thin slices of brown bread and butter. Selection of small cakes and cream meringues. Shortbread, Chocolate and Fruit Cake. Earl Grey or Indian tea with lemon.

KITCHEN CUPPA

Toasted Tea Cakes

Buttered Toast with Honey

Bread and Butter with Jam or Paste

Chocolate Cake, Fruit Cake, etc.

Lots of Tea, Herbal or otherwise

ENGLISH CREAM TEA consisting of:-

Scones, Jam and Cream — can be served at either Afternoon Tea or Kitchen Cuppa.

DINNERS

The suggested Menus below are for special occasions, though of course you can have a 'mad moment' and do something special just because class went well, or you did a "perfect pirouette", or just because you feel like it.

Lay the table attractively, offer wine or fruit juice.

1. Mushrooms in Brandy (p.186)
   Fresh Salmon Steaks with Soured Cream (p.60)
   New Potatoes
   Mange Tout or Peas

   Crepe Suzette or Syllabub (p.165 & p.166)
   Cheeseboard & Biscuits
   Coffee

OR

2. Caviar
   Beef Wellington (p.177)
   Sauté Potatoes
   Spinach & Carrots

   Pavlova or Sorbet (p.150)

   Potted Stilton (p.186)
   Stuffed Grapes
   Coffee

SUPPERS

At the end of a long day or rehearsals or before a show, when a friend drops in. When you are too tired to get much else. Suppers can fit any time for anybody or manybodies. Suggestions only.

1. Soup, with chunks of wholemeal bread
   Pancakes with Chocolate Sauce or Lemon
   Cheese & Biscuits
   Coffee, Tea, Beer or Wine

2. Ratatouille, French Bread (p.78)
   Apple Cake or Apple Fritters (p.99)
   Cheese & Biscuits
   Coffee, Tea, Beer or Wine

3. Mince, potatoes, sprouts, carrots (p.38)
   Quick American Cheesecake (p.103)
   Cheese, raw vegetables
   Coffee, Tea, Beer or Wine

4. Stir Fried Prawns & Broccoli (p.54)
   Apricot Fool (p.128)
   Cheese & Biscuits
   Coffee or Tea

5. Grilled Fresh Fish, new potatoes, mixed salad
   Dutch Delight (p.152)
   Cheeses
   Coffee or Tea

Beef Wellington

600g/1½lb Fillet Beef
25g/1oz Mushrooms
50g/2oz Fine textured Pâté
1 small Onion
1 clove Garlic
2 tsp Brandy
Salt and Black Pepper
25g/1oz Butter

Pastry

400g/1lb frozen Puff Pastry or make pastry (which can be made day before)
200g/½lb plain flour
200g/½lb butter (or half & half butter and lard)
2 tsp lemon juice
Cold water to mix

Oven: Gas no. 7. 425°F. 220°C. for 20 mins, then
Gas no. 4. 350°F. 180°C. for 15 mins.

Baking Sheet

Method

1. Trim any fat from beef, rub the brandy, cut garlic and salt & pepper into the beef if it needs it — tie string round to keep it to a sausage shape.
2. Heat butter in thick fry pan, put beef in, brown quickly each side to seal, then reduce heat. Cook approximately 20 minutes — turning regularly. Do not overcook, better undercook.
3. Remove and put on plate to get completely cold.

***Pastry* — or use Frozen Puff Pastryy**

1. Sift flour into bowl, add ¼ of the butter into flour, rub into flour, bind with the lemon juice — add water if not enough juice.
2. Roll out pastry on floured board, spread remaining butter over pastry, fold each end over, then sides over, till a parcel. Seal edges by pressing together.
3. Now turn pastry — roll out again to oblong shape, three times larger than wide. Fold bottom up halfway, top down. Repeat this sequence 2 or 3 times, working gently and quickly. Wrap pastry in clingfilm, put in fridge 30 minutes.
4. Chop onion and mushroom finely, sauté briefly — 5 minutes.
5. Roll out pastry so that is is wider than the piece of beef, and twice as long.
6. Remove string from beef, lay it on the pastry. Spread the pâté on top of meat, then mushroom and onion on top of pâté.
7. Fold long end over till it meets other end. Seal edges well. Cut 2 or 3 diagonal slits in top of pastry, brush with beaten egg, cut pastry leaves to decorate.
8. Place on floured baking tray.

Cook as instructions — do not overcook.

Transfer to warm serving dish and garnish with parsley.

Steak au Poivre

4 rump steaks (or however many are needed) approx 150g/6oz each
Black peppercorns (about 4 per steak)
Garlic butter (see Dressing Up section)

Method

1. Crush peppercorns using a plastic bag and rolling pin. Put them crushed, onto a flat surface.
2. Trim steaks, press each side into the peppercorns, sprinkle on salt — leave to stand for ½ hour.
3. Oil the grill pan, get hot. Put steaks under grill, turning to seal each side, reduce heat, cook to desired choice.

N.B. see cooking times on page 202.

Chicken Madeira

600g/1 ½lb boned chicken breasts
50g/2oz butter
30ml/1 fl.oz. oil
1 onion, chopped
1 clove garlic, crushed
4 tbsp madeira (or sherry)
280ml/10oz double cream
Salt & black pepper
Thin orange & lemon slices to decorate

Method

1. Cut the chicken pieces into slices about 6mm/ ¼" thick, dip in seasoned flour.
2. Heat butter & oil in pan, add chopped onion and garlic, sauté a few minutes.
3. Put onion & garlic to side of pan, now add chicken pieces, sauté both sides until sealed.
4. Now put in madeira (or sherry), cook over fairly high heat — about 15 - 20 minutes.
5. Add cream, stir for a few minutes.
6. Serve garnished with lemon and orange slices.

Lasagne

100g/4oz lasagne verdi
12g/½oz butter
400g/1lb minced beef
1 clove garlic
3 rashers streaky bacon
1 onion, peeled and chopped
2 carrots, peeled and grated
280ml/½ pint beef stock
2 tbsp tomato purée
Salt & black pepper
Pinch nutmeg

Cheese Sauce

50g/2oz margarine
50g/2oz plain flour
570ml/1 pint milk
150g/6oz strong cheddar cheese
Parmesan cheese for top

Oven: Gas no. 5. 375°F. 190°C. 25 minutes
4 pint ovenproof dish

Method

1. Bring pan of salted water to boil, add leaves of lasagne one at a time to prevent sticking. Cook for 15 minutes, drain, separate on a plate and leave on one side.
2. Chop bacon into small pieces, put in with the butter, crushed garlic and chopped onion. Cook over fairly hot heat until soft.
3. Add minced beef, carrots, tomato purée, stock and seasoning. Bring to the boil, mixing all together, lower heat, simmer for 30 minutes.

Cheese Sauce

1. Melt margarine in pan, add flour, then a little milk. Gradually add rest of milk stirring all the time until thick and creamy. Now add cheese and seasoning, cook for 5 minutes, remove from heat.

Grease the ovenproof dish, cover base with layer of lasagne, then some of the meat mixture, then cheese sauce. Repeat layers once more, finishing with cheese sauce.

Sprinkle a little extra cheese on top and the pinch of nutmeg. Put in oven, cook until golden brown.

Note: You can now buy lasagne that does not need pre-cooking.

Seafood Platter

With this dish, you can be as extravagant or as modest as you wish.

Serve on a large meat dish, or flat plate. Cover base with washed and dried lettuce and spinach leaves, or make a bed of fresh herbs.

Arrange the seafood in circles attractively, using all, or a selection from:-

Prawns, brown shrimps, crayfish, lobster tails or pieces of lobster, cockles, whelks, winkles, oysters.

Serve with thin brown bread and butter and lemon wedges.

Prawn Cocktail

6 lettuce leaves, washed, dried and shredded finely
200g/8oz peeled prawns (well thawed if using frozen)
1 tsp lemon juice

Sauce

140ml/ ¼ pint made mayonnaise
4 tbsp tomato ketchup
Dash tabasco
Dash worcester sauce
Salt & black pepper

Method

Sauce

1. Place all sauce ingredients together. Mix well.
2. Put shredded lettuce into individual glasses.
3. Drain prawns and pat dry.
4. Place prawns into a bowl, squeeze lemon juice over, then the sauce. Mix well, but gently.
5. Divide the mixture between glasses, garnish with slice of lemon.

Salmon Mousse (serves 6 - 8)

420g/15oz can red salmon
140ml/¼ pint double cream
140ml/¼ pint milk stock (I use ½ the juice from salmon made up with water)
140ml/ ¼ pint mayonnaise
Juice of 1 lemon
Pinch of paprika, salt & black pepper
1 small onion, chopped finely
140ml/¼ pint water
3 tsp powdered gelatine

2 pint mould

Method

1. Put water into a small pan. Put gelatine in and give time to dissolve, then heat gently until completely dissolved. Stir in stock, leave to cool.
2. Mix together mayonnaise, lemon juice, seasoning and onion.
3. Strain the gelatine into the mixture.
4. Flake salmon, fold into mixture, then fold in cream.
5. Turn into dampened mould. Chill until firm.
6. Turn mould upside down onto a serving plate. Decorate mousse with slices of cucumber.

If mousse sticks, immerse bottom of mould into bowl of hot water for a second to loosen.

Potted Stilton

50g/2oz butter
200g/ ½lb stilton — or use left over stilton pieces
1 tbsp port

Method

1. Mash together the softened butter & stilton. When well combined add the Port, mix well.
2. Put into china pot, smooth top, cover with clingfilm, put to chill.

This is nice to serve as a little luxury at the end of the meal, with water biscuits.

Mushrooms in Brandy

200g/8oz button mushrooms
1 tbsp brandy
1 tbsp olive oil
3 tbsp white wine
1 small onion
Salt & black pepper
Small carton double cream
Pinch mustard

Method

1. Trim mushrooms, chop onion.
2. Put onion, oil, brandy and white wine in pan. Heat through, then add mushrooms and simmer for 10 minutes
3. Put in a basin, leave in fridge overnight.
4. Drain off liquid (keep this for a soup or sauce).
5. Put mustard with cream, spoon over top of mushrooms — garnish with chopped parsley.

ACT 2

SCENE 5

CHOCOLATE REVÈRÉNCE

REVERIE

How apt I thought to end this Cookery Book for Dancers with luscious chocolate recipes. Immediately the title "Chocolate Reverence" seemed appropriate, being an acknowledgement to chocolate, and the end of the book.

As a great lover of chocolate myself, but only able to tolerate it in small quantities due to migraine, my one piece at a time gives pleasure which I am sure surpasses that experienced by the pure indulgers.

I hope the slimmers will win this battle of mind over matter, and derive the anticipated delight in their small ration, then without envy of those who can eat their fill, join together as we lose ourselves in a "Reverie to Chocolate".

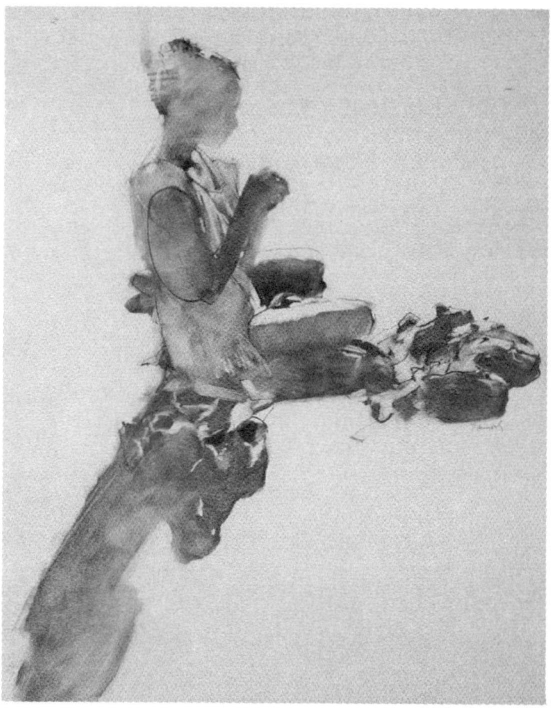

Chocolate Pâté

Starter for Chocolate Freaks

100g/4oz bitter chocolate
100g/4oz milk chocolate
140ml/¼ pint double cream
50g/2oz butter
50g/2oz chopped nuts
1 tsp coffee liqueur (optional)

Method

1. Melt chocolate in a bowl over hot water.
2. Place cream in a saucepan and heat to just below boiling point. Remove from heat.
3. Add melted chocolate and butter. Stir briskly.
4. When mixture has thickened and cooled stir in nut & liqueur.
5. Spoon into a pâté dish, press down, cover with cling film.

Serve at room temperature.

Note: If too firm add a little more cream.

This is the starter for "Chocolate Freaks". Arrange a plate of sliced oranges, or fruit of your choice and chocolate wholemeal biscuits with the pâté.

Chocolate Omelette

Main course for Chocolate Freaks

2 eggs
1tsp cocoa powder
Butter for cooking
1 heaped tbsp chocolate ice cream

Method

1. Whisk egg whites until stiff & holding peaks.
2. Beat egg yolks, add cocoa powder. Fold in gently.
3. Melt butter in omelette pan.
4. Fold egg whites into egg yolk and cocoa mixture.
5. Cook as normal omelette.
6. At last moment put tbsp of chocolate ice cream onto omelette. Fold over — serve at once.

Chocolate Salad

2 or 3 small, firm lettuce leaves (use same day)
1 eating apple
Small bunch grapes
100g/4oz dark cooking chocolate

Method

1. Melt chocolate in bowl over saucepan of hot water.
2. With a pastry brush coat lettuce leaves with melted chocolate — does not matter if streaks of green lettuce show through. Put to dry, resting over something — like bottom of cup.
3. Leave skin on an apple, remove core and cut into slices. Leave grapes whole.
4. Dip the fruit into melted chocolate. Leave on a wire rack or smooth surface to harden. 2 — 3 hours.
5. Serve chocolate fruit on bed of chocolate lettuce leaves.

It is refreshing to serve PLAIN fresh fruit — grapes, orange segments and perhaps pieces of cucumber and slivers of raw carrot to compliment the chocolate.

Chocolate Roulade

Sweet for Chocolate Freaks

150g/6oz plain dark chocolate
5 eggs
125g/5oz caster sugar
2 tbsp hot water
280ml/½ pint double cream — whipped until thick
Icing sugar for dusting

Oven: Gas no. 5. 190°F. 375°C. 15 - 20 minutes
Swiss roll tin

Method

1. Melt chocolate in bowl over hot water.
2. Separate eggs, combine the yolks & caster sugar. Beat until pale & creamy. Add melted chocolate and hot water.
3. Whisk egg whites until stiff — fold into mixture.
4. Brush tin with melted butter and line with greaseproof paper.
5. Pour mixture into tin — smooth.
6. Put to bake — when done, remove from oven and leave overnight (having made sure cake is loose in tin).
7. Spread chocolate base with whipped double cream and roll up, using greaseproof paper to help.
8. Place on a serving dish, dust with icing sugar. Decorate modestly or lavishly with chocolate flakes.

Chocolate Shortbread

For Chocolate Freaks

150g/6oz plain flour
100g/4oz butter
50g/2oz caster sugar
12g/½oz cocoa powder

Oven: Gas no. 4. 180°F. 350°C. 30 minutes.
Baking tin 11" x 7"

Method

1. Sift together flour and cocoa. Rub in butter until mixture is like breadcrumbs.
2. Add sugar, mix to a smooth dough.
3. Press the mixture into a lightly greased tin.
4. Bake.

Cool in tin, cut into squares or fingers.

Dark Chocolate Fudge

400g/1lb sugar
6 tbsp milk
25g/1oz butter
150g/6oz plain dark chocolate

Lightly greased 8" square tin

Method

1. Place all ingredients in a pan. Put on low heat and stir until dissolved and the chocolate melted.
2. Bring to boil, boil until mixture reaches 240°F. 115°C., using a thermometer, or until a little dropped into cold water forms a ball.
3. Remove from heat. Beat until mixture thickens.
4. Pour into tin, leave to get cold. Cut into 1" (2.5cm) squares.

You can add 1 tbsp rum essence with the other ingredients if you want a rum flavour.

Grande Cheesecake

200g/8oz digestive biscuits (crushed)
100g/4oz butter
140ml/¼ pint sour cream
400g/1lb curd or cream cheese
1 tbsp lemon juice
6 tbsp caster sugar
2 egg yolks
50g/2oz dark chocolate
1 tsp vanilla essence
3 tbsp grand marnier (or any favourite liqueur)

Oven: Gas no. ½. 250°F. 130°C.
Loose bottom 8" cake tin

Method

Grease a loose bottom 8" cake tin. Melt butter in saucepan. Add crushed biscuit crumbs, mix well, and press into bottom of cake tin.

Blend together cream cheese and ⅔ of sour cream. Add lemon juice, 4 tbsp caster sugar, vanilla essence and egg yolks. Beat until smooth and divide in half, putting in separate containers. Melt chocolate in bowl over hot water. Cool, then add to one half of the cheese mixture. Into the other half add the Grand Marnier (or other liqueur). Pour chocolate half on to biscuit base, then the liqueur half on top. Blend together remaining ⅓ sour cream and caster sugar — spread over top of cheesecake. Bake 20 minutes. When chilled, cover top with thickly grated chocolate.

Chocolate Pears

4 ripe pears — with stalks
100g/4oz dark plain chocolate
2 eggs
25g/1oz butter
3 tbsp cold black coffee
1 tbsp rum or brandy (or essence)
12g/½oz glacé cherries
12g/½oz chopped nuts
Strip of angelica for garnishing — optional.

Method

1. Peel pears very carefully and thinly. Cut out core from base, but leave stem at top intact.
2. Chop cherries, mix with nuts and stuff this in the pear, where you took the core out.
3. Stand pears up in serving dish.
4. Break up chocolate, put in a bowl with the coffee. Stand over a saucepan of hot water until chocolate has melted. Remove from heat and add butter and rum or essence.
5. Separate eggs, beat yolks into chocolate mixture.
6. Whisk egg white, fold into mixture.
7. Spoon this mixture over pears until they are evenly coated. Chill overnight in fridge. If desired, cut angelica into strips and decorate pears at top where the stalks are.

Serve with cream.

Chocolate Fudge Cake

3 tbsp cocoa powder
100g/4oz margarine
120ml/4 fl.oz. oil
240ml/8 fl.oz. water
300g/12oz caster sugar
2 eggs
120ml/4oz milk
1 tsp vanilla essence
¼ tsp bicarbonate of soda

Icing

3 tbsp cocoa powder
100g/4oz margarine
400g/1lb icing sugar
90ml/3oz evaporated milk

Oven: Gas no. 4. 350°F. 180°C. 1 - 1½ hours

2lb loaf tin

Method

1. Place cocoa, margarine, oil and water in a pan. Bring to boil, remove from heat, cool slightly.
2. Stir in caster sugar and sifted flour.
3. Beat together egg, milk and bicarbonate of soda. Add to mixture.
4. Grease and line the tin.
5. Put mixture into tin, bake. When cooked turn onto wire rack to cool.

Icing

Put all ingredients into a pan, gently bring to boil. Beat well until smooth and shiny. Pour over the cooled cake while still warm.

Moist Chocolate Cake

100g/4oz plain flour
12g/½oz cocoa powder
½ level tsp baking powder
50g/2oz butter
50g/2oz caster sugar
100g/4oz golden syrup
1 egg
3 tbsp milk

Fudge Frosting

100g/4oz icing sugar
25g/1oz cocoa powder
50g/2oz butter
2 tbsp water
50g/2oz caster sugar
Few drops of vanilla essence

Oven: Gas no. 4. 350°F. 180°C. 30 - 35 minutes
7" square tin

Method

1. Grease and line baking tin.
2. Sift flour, baking powder and cocoa into a bowl.
3. Put butter, golden syrup and sugar into a saucepan. Stir over heat until ingredients have melted and combined. Put to cool.
4. Mix together egg and milk, add to melted ingredients.
5. Pour into sifted flour and mix well.
6. Spoon into tin, spread evenly and bake.

Fudge Frosting overleaf...

Fudge Frosting

1. Sift icing sugar and cocoa into mixing bowl.
2. Put butter, water and sugar into a saucepan. Heat gently, stirring until dissolved and just boiling — remove from heat.
3. Pour hot syrup into sieved ingredients, mix well to make a smooth coating. Keep beating until frosting is thick enough to coat cake.
4. Pour over cake. Leave standing until frosting has set.

Chocolate Meringue

100g/4oz dark plain chocolate
1 pint milk
3 eggs
2 tsp caster sugar
40g/1½oz icing sugar

Oven: Gas no. 3. 325°F. 170°C. 1 - 1¼ hours
1 pint ovenproof dish

Method

1. Break chocolate, put with milk in saucepan stirring to dissolve completely.
2. Beat one whole egg and 2 egg yolks with the caster sugar in a bowl, then pour on the warm milk, stirring well.
3. Lightly grease ovenproof dish. Pour chocolate custard in through a sieve. Place dish in a baking tin half filled with water.
4. When custard is cooked you will tell by the fact it is set.
5. Whisk 2 remaining egg whites with the sieved sugar until holding peaks. Put this on top of set custard. Put under hot grill to just brown the meringue. Sprinkle with chopped nuts or chocolate flakes.

Chocolate Romance

100g/4oz plain chocolate drops
2 eggs
140ml/5oz soured cream (or plain yogurt) — see note
50g/2oz plain dark chocolate

Method

1. Melt chocolate drops in basin over hot water. Stir occasionally until melted, remove from heat.
2. Add egg yolks to cooled melted chocolate. Beat until smooth.
3. Whip soured cream until holding peaks. Stir 4 tbsp into chocolate.
4. Whisk egg whites until stiff. Fold into chocolate mixture with metal spoon.
5. Divide mixture between 4 serving dishes or glasses. Chill until set.
6. Melt plain dark chocolate and spread onto a smooth surface. When cold use a heart shaped cutter (or draw the shape of hearts). Cut 4 heart shapes.
7. Put remaining soured cream or yogurt on top of chocolate mixture, then lay a chocolate heart on the cream.

Note: If using yogurt it is best not to beat it — just use straight from the carton. Does not make such a thick mixture as the soured cream.

Chocolate Crumblies

150g/6oz butter
4 tbsp drinking chocolate powder
2 tbsp golden syrup
1 lemon
1 pkt digestive biscuits (12oz)
2 bars Aero chocolate or milk chocolate of any sort

10" x 6" shallow cake tin

Method

1. Place butter, chocolate powder, syrup and finely grated lemon rind in a pan. Heat slowly until butter has melted, remove from heat.
2. Crush biscuits in a mixer, or in a polythene bag using a rolling pin. Stir crumbs into melted mixture.
3. Put mixture into cake tin — pressing down well. Put in fridge for approximately 1 hour.
4. Melt Aero bars, spread roughly over top — leave to set, then cut into squares.

Chocolate Creams (makes approx 6)

150g/6oz dark chocolate
280ml/½ pint double cream
1 egg
½ tsp vanilla essence

Method

1. Break chocolate, put in liquidizer.
2. Heat cream until almost boiling — pour over chocolate. Switch on and blend until chocolate melted.
3. Beat egg, add to mixture with vanilla essence, blend.
4. Pour into individual dishes. Chill overnight.

Smooth, creamy, delicious.

Conversion Table

These are approximate conversions, but right for the recipes. Never mix the two systems. Use either Metric or British.

Spoon measurements — level.

Weight

British	Metric	American Equivalent
¼oz	10g	½ cup gound nuts
1oz	25g	1 cup grated cheese
2ozs	50g	½ cup dried fruit
4ozs	110g	⅔ cup brown sugar
6ozs	175g	1½ cups icing sugar
8ozs	225g	1½ cups coarse meals
16oz (1lb)	450g	2 cups butter or marg
3lbs	1kg 350g	4 cups flour, white sugar

Volume

British	Metric	American
1fl.oz	30mls	2 Tbsp.
2fl.ozs	70mls	¼ cup
5fl.ozs (¼ pt)	150mls	⅔ cup
10fl.ozs (½ pt)	300mls	1¼ cups
20fl.ozs (1pt)	575mls	2½ cups
1¾ pints	1 litre	4½ cups

Oven Temperatures

GAS	- ½	1	2	3	4	5	6	7	8	9
°F.	- 250	275	300	325	350	375	400	425	450	475
°C.	- 130	140	150	170	180	190	200	220	230	240

As my performance comes to a close,

Bouquets of thanks go the Principals:

David, Graham, Cherry
Philip Arnott
Jim Penwarden
Tony Birks-Hay

also, the Corps-de-Helpers

Alice Finch-Hatton
Ashley Thompson
Len Copeland
Andrew Crane

Ray, Sarah and Giles and many friends for their encouragement.

Finally, to Dancers and Cookery Book lovers everywhere

The Dancers Own Cookbook